Leaning on the Moment

Leaning
on the
Moment

Interviews from PARABOLA

PARABOLA BOOKS
New York, N.Y.

PARABOLA BOOKS are published by the Society for the Study of Myth and Tradition, a not-for-profit organization devoted to the dissemination and exploration of materials relating to myth, symbol, ritual, and art of the great religious traditions. The Society also publishes PARABOLA, The Quarterly Magazine of Myth and Tradition.

LEANING ON THE MOMENT
A Parabola Book/November 1986

Book design by Gloria Claudia Ortíz

ISBN: 0-930407-02-4

Parabola Books
656 Broadway
New York, N.Y. 10012

PRINTED IN THE UNITED STATES OF AMERICA

Contents

Foreword

In its dozen years of hardworking life, PARABOLA Magazine has had one always reliable source of pleasure and profit in its opportunities to meet and converse with some of the most interesting people of our times. We have published an interview with one of them in nearly every issue, and in some issues, more than one (there were eight in our Tenth Anniversary number on "Wholeness"). Since each of PARABOLA's four annual issues examines a different central theme, we seek out a person with some special knowledge of or connection with it, and these talks have evidently been stimulating to the people we have interviewed as well as to us. They have brought us so much rich material on each issue's main subject, as well as on the present relevance and immediate importance of our central themes of myth and tradition, that we have made a selection of them to publish in book form.

The majority of the conversations recorded here were conducted by one or more of the magazine's editorial staff as it has changed over the years, and who appear in the conversation simply as "PARABOLA." These past or present staff members are Susan Bergholz, D.M. Dooling, Lorraine Kisly, Jeff Zaleski, and Philip Zaleski. Other interviewers are distinguished by name and some biographical data. We wish also to mention with special thanks the help we have received on many occasions from Professor Robert A.F. Thurman of Amherst College in facilitating, interpreting, and translating conversations with visitors from Tibet.

Some of these interviews took place a number of years ago, and we have updated information and references in them as necessary. The first interview, with Professor Eliade, appeared in our second issue, in 1976. We reprint it now in the year of his death, with a very special feeling of gratitude and of our and the world's loss in his departure. He was one of PARABOLA's first friends and consultants when the magazine only existed as an idea and a hope.

Our thanks are due once again to all the people with whom we have talked over the years, who have given us generously of their thought, their time, and their attention. We feel them all as our appreciated friends. It was not easy to choose among them, and we have consoled ourselves for certain omissions with the possibility of another volume later. In any case, we offer this one for the enjoyment of our readers with unquestioning confidence in the quality of the feast that awaits them.

The Editors

1

♦

An Interview with Mircea Eliade

"Initiation," VOL. 1:3, May, 1976

Initiation

Mircea Eliade, scholar, novelist, and playwright, world authority on the history of religions, was born in Bucharest in 1907. After travels and studies in Europe and India, and some years of teaching at the Sorbonne in Paris, he came in 1957 to the University of Chicago where he remained until his death in April of 1986. He headed the University's department of religions, later became the Sewell Avery Distinguished Service Professor at the Divinity School, and there is now a chair named for him in the History of Religions department.

When PARABOLA began to exist as a still-unrealized idea, it was natural to seek out a man so famous in the field we were proposing to enter and to ask for his blessing. We went to meet him with a preconceived image suggested by his learning, his formidable vocabulary, and the number and profundity of his books: the high-browed, absent-minded professor, some sort of august rat de bibliothèque heavily endowed with academic honors. So it was a surprise to meet this rather sprightly and certainly humorous and charming person; professorial perhaps, but absent-minded, no. His eyes were keen as well as kindly behind his glasses, and he gave the very strong impression of a man who knows what is going on. His office, as one might have expected, was lined with books; not only from floor to ceiling, but from wall to wall. Books, papers, and periodicals were literally stacked; neither the desk nor the floor were visible, their presences were merely inferred. But in the course of our conversation he would frequently mention a book or a magazine article: "It is right here, I believe," and there it would be, fourth from the top in the third stack due north of the window.

But it was not only the precision and the wide-ranging quality of his mind that

3

one felt in talking with him, or in reading his work; what gave his words their particular weight is that behind the scholar was a man whose life had been molded by the "sacred" of which he speaks. He insisted on the title of "religious historian," as if he wished to protect something within those safe limits. But he was much more; he was also, and more importantly, a man of religion.

♦

PARABOLA The word "initiation" today refers mostly to college hazing or entering a Lodge; but what is its real, traditional significance?

MIRCEA ELIADE In the most general sense, the term denotes a body of rites and oral teachings whose purpose is to produce a radical modification of the religious and social status of the person to be initiated. Initiation is such an experience that the novice emerges from his ordeal a totally different and transformed being who will never be the same again.

Broadly, we can point to three different types of initiation: initiations into adulthood, into secret societies, and into mystical vocations. Each has its own special characteristics—for instance, the prevalence of the ecstatic element in the initiations of mystical vocations—but there is a sort of common denominator among all these categories, with the result that from a certain point of view all initiations are much alike.

P. Is there anything in our religious or social life today, in the education of young people or in the training for special professions, that can be thought of as initiatic?

M.E. Initiatory themes remain alive chiefly in modern man's unconscious. This is confirmed not only by the initiatory symbolism of certain artistic creations—poems, novels, films, and works of plastic art—but also by the reception of these works by the public. Just think of the enormous success of Jules Verne's novels, the initiatory structure of which has been brilliantly analyzed by Simone Vierve in her book, *Jules Verne et le roman initiatique*. Other writers have recognized initiatory scenarios in *Moby Dick*, *Walden*, *Huckleberry Finn*, Faulkner's *The Bear*, as well as in the work of such diverse authors as James Fenimore Cooper, Henry James, Sherwood Anderson, F. Scott Fitzgerald, and Thomas Wolfe. The fact that artistic representation of initiatic theses can find massive, spontaneous acceptance certainly indicates that in the depths of his being, modern man is still capable of being moved by initiatory scenarios or messages.

P. Would you say that initiation is fundamental to all religions, or are there initiatic and non-initiatic religions, and how, essentially, would they differ?

M.E. All religions possess a fundamental initiatory scenario but its importance varies widely from one type of religion to another and from one historical moment to another. In the last two centuries, for example, Christian initiation has almost disappeared. But from the first, Christian baptism was equivalent to an initiation. Baptism introduced the convert to a new religious community and made him worthy of eternal life. The Church Fathers emphasized its initiatory function, continually multiplying images of death and resurrection. The baptismal font itself was often compared to both the tomb and the womb, being at one time the tomb in which the catechumen buries his earthly life and the womb in which the eternal life is born. Another cultic act that is initiatory in structure is the Eucharist, instituted by Jesus at the Last Supper. Through this rite, the Christian shares in the body and blood of his Savior. By the fourth century, the constitution of the *arcana disciplina*, the "secret teachings," is complete. In other words, it had been decided that the Christian mysteries were to be guarded from the uninitiated. The Pseudo-Areopagite warns the Christian initiate—who has experienced the divine mystagogy—to keep silence: "Take care that you do not reveal the holy of holies, preserve the mysteries of the hidden God so that the profane may not partake of them and in your sacred illumination speak of the sacred only to saints" (i.e., the "Christian initiates").

But the various Christian denominations no longer appreciate the initiatory values of their cultic acts. In the last two centuries, the theologians—particularly among Protestant denominations—have emphasized the philosophical, social, and ethical values of Christianity, ignoring its initiatory dimension. This is perhaps due to the apparently "undemocratic" intent of initiation—since any initiation implies a selection.

P. Then Christian esotericism has disappeared along with initiation? Where did it go? Might it still be found at Mount Athos, for instance?

There is confusion about the real meaning of esotericism. How would you explain it? In fact, we see many terms in common use that are very vaguely defined in practice. What, for instance, is religion? Or tradition? And what is the difference between them?

M.E. The simplest definition of esotericism is, in my opinion, a secret corpus of doctrines, rituals, and spiritual techniques regarded as revealed in primordial times by Supernatural Beings, and transmitted by means of specific initiation to a limited number of disciples. In every religion we find a large *exoteric* set of beliefs, rituals, and theological formulae and, concomitantly, their *esoteric* interpretation. The term "tradition" is usually employed with relation to an esoteric understanding of a particular religion. However, "tradition" and "traditional" are also used to designate any authentic, not yet acculturated type of culture, religion, or society.

P. Another term that we would like your help in defining is myth itself. What really is myth, as differentiated from folktale, parable, fable, epic? Are there "modern myths"—do new myths emerge, or are they simply old ones in new clothing? How does myth actually operate in our times?

M.E. Myth is an extremely complex cultural reality which can be approached and interpreted from various and complementary viewpoints. Speaking for myself, the definition which seems least inadequate and most embracing is this: any myth tells *how something came into being*—the world, man, animal species, social institutions, and so on. Myth, then, is always an account of a "creation"; it relates how something was produced or began to *be*. The actors in myths are Supernatural Beings. They are known primarily by what they did in the mythical times of the "beginnings." Hence myths disclose the creative activity of these beings and reveal the sacredness (or "supernaturalness") of their work. For this reason, myth becomes the *exemplary model* for all significant human activity. In traditional societies, myths are considered "true stories," and as such are carefully distinguished from fables or tales, which are called "false stories."

Some forms of "mythical behavior" still survive in our days. I have discussed a number of "myths of the modern world" in my book *Myth and Reality*. Of course it is difficult to summarize the long analysis given there in an adequate fashion. To give only a few examples, though, one can discover the mythical structure of Marx's classless society and the consequent disappearance of all historical tensions after the triumph of the proletariat: the "Aryan purity and perfection" exalted by Nazism is equally a mythological construction, shrewdly adapted for specific political objectives. One can also see how much the images and behavior patterns imposed on large numbers of people by the mass media correspond to specific mythical structures. The sociologist of religion Andrew Greeley has correctly and humorously described the "cult of the sacred automobile" in contemporary American society. But even the *intelligentsia* experiences the fascination of mythical behavior. There are a number of "myths of the elite" that merit study. For instance, the redeeming function of "difficulty," especially as found in works of modern art. If the elite revel in *Finnegan's Wake*, in atonal music, or in the latest expressions of nonfigurative arts, it is largely because such works represent closed worlds, hermetic universes that cannot be entered except by overcoming immense difficulties, like the initiation ordeals of the archaic and traditional societies. The *cognoscenti* proclaim to the "others" (i.e, the "mass") that they belong to a select minority, to a gnosis that has the advantage of being at once spiritual and secular.

P. As an historian of religions, you are no doubt able to see the historical place of the present-day interests in all kinds of religious teachings and practices. What do you consider the causes of this phenomenon?

M.E. Most of these teachings and practices express the rebellion of youth against the institutionalized religions of the so-called "establishment." The main cause of this phenomenon is, it seems to me, the unbearable experience of a religious void. Because the younger generations cannot grasp any longer the meaning of Jewish and Christian symbols and rituals, they search for meaning and spiritual help in the Oriental religions, especially in some eccentric neo-Asiatic cultural vogues. No less significant for a historian of religions is the kind of neopaganism much in favor with the younger generation: the rediscovery of "cosmic religion" and the sacramental dimensions of human existence—for instance, communion with nature, ritual nudity, uninhibited sexual spontaneity, the will to live exclusively in the present, and so on.

P. But in spite of this widespread interest in religion, it seems that traditional ideas take no part in contemporary life. If we speak of a traditional society as one in which another level of reality, which might be called the sacred, is recognized as the real point of reference for everything that takes place on the ordinary plane, we certainly can't call our society a traditional one. What would you say about that?

M.E. By definition, *traditional* ideas cannot play a role in *modern* societies.

However, in the last few years we have begun to witness a growing and ever more competent criticism of "modern life" directed from different traditional perspectives. This is particularly true in Europe.

P. You have said, however, that modern man has lost the dimension of the sacred. Do you feel that we live in a dark age, religiously speaking—Kali Yuga, as some say—a time that is unfavorable for a real spiritual search?

M.E. Yes, "modern man" has lost the dimension of the sacred. Of course, however, I do not include those who *believe*, *practice*, and *ponder* their own religious heritage within the rubric of "modern men." But even the nonreligious Western man still dreams, reads novels and poetry, listens to music, goes to the theater, loves "Nature," and so forth. And this means that *unconsciously* he communicates with the sacred. I must add, however, that the problem is too complex to be solved in a few sentences. For this reason I am somewhat reluctant to discuss such delicate problems in an interview; they are difficult enough to investigate even in a long essay . . . .

P. Do you see any hope of a return to traditional values? Would such a hope reside in a return to separate teachings or "churches," or in the discovery of a central, source teaching which is perhaps the root of all the others?

M.E. In the world of the spirit, *everything* is possible. But I would not dare to utter oracular predictions. Most probably there will be a kind of "opening" in the great religions, a growing interest in the "universalistic" values discovered in religious traditions that have been heretofore considered "heretic," "pagan," or even "diabolic."

P. Do you believe there is such a central tradition which has found different cultural expressions in different times and places?

M.E. There is, certainly, a central tradition, which different cultures inherited from at least the neolithic era. That is to say, a certain number of fundamental concepts related to man's discovery of his own mode of being were transmitted from generation to generation. Although the expressions of this understanding differ, the theoretical content is largely the same.

P. You have been criticized on occasion for drawing your view of the nature of religion primarily from primitive religions rather than from the full spectrum of religious traditions. How would you respond? In particular, you say in *The Sacred and the Profane*: "Acting as a fully responsible human being, man imitates the paradigmatic gestures of the gods, repeats their actions. . . . " In what sense is this true of such contemporary religions as Christianity, Islam, and Buddhism?

M.E. I have insisted upon the importance of primitive religions because they were more or less neglected by historians of religions in the past. The most important books on this problem were written by anthropologists and sociologists such as Frazer, Durkheim, Lévy-Bruhl, Wilhelm Schmidt, Robert Lowie, Malinowski, Paul Radin, and others.

Now, with regard to the imitation of paradigmatic models revealed by Supernatural Beings, there is a linear continuity between the archaic, "primitive" religions and the so-called high religions. In Christianity, Islam, or Buddhism, we do find the same basic principle: *imitatio dei*. The faithful repeat the exemplary *gesta* of their model. The ideal Christian— i.e., the Saint—is one who achieves the most fully an *imitatio Christi*. The ultimate goal of every Buddhist is *nirvana*, and he knows that he will attain *nirvana* only through a perfect "imitation" of his model, Gautama Buddha.

P. It is sometimes said that magic is, as it were, the technique or science of religion, both religion and magic together being the indispensable elements of a tradition. It seems that alchemy might be thought of as part of this magical aspect of religion. In *The Forge and the Crucible* you speak of the belief of the alchemists that the process of the transmutation of metals was simultaneously a process of self-perfecting or transformation of being. Do you think the operational side of alchemy was purely symbolic?

M.E. The operational side of alchemy was *ritual*, and as such, symbolic. This means that the alchemist was operating simultaneously on physical matter and on his own "human condition"; the processes which were intended to effect the transmutation of metals concomitantly realized a radical transformation of the alchemist's mode of being.

P. In the last chapter of the same book, you make some tantalizing statements that we would like to ask you to amplify. You say: "The secularization of work is like an open wound in the body of modern society. There is, however, nothing to indicate that a *re-sanctification may not take place in the future*. As to the temporality of the human condition, it presents an even more serious discovery. But a reconciliation with temporality remains a possibility, *given a more correct conception of time*."
Will you say more about that?

M.E. I still think that the "re-sanctification" of work is possible. There are a number of recent examples of voluntary, "spontaneous" labor undertaken in the name of an *ideal* (even a political cause!). This labor was effectuated with joy, and none of the workers ever felt the *burden of time*. I have known many "volunteers" in Mahatma Gandhi's nonviolent campaigns (for instance, extracting salt from the sea to avoid the British-imposed tax on salt) who could work between sixteen and eighteen hours a day, singing, laughing, and shouting out of sheer joy. I have also met some sincere Communists who, so long as they thought they were "building a new type of society," were neither tired nor oppressed by the *burden of time*, not even after ten or twelve hours of hard work in a factory. Any type of labor that is undertaken for an *ideal* such as defense or liberation of one's own country, preaching a religious, social, or ethical message, and so on, can be performed in a kind of "ecstatic" enthusiasm—one might also say, "outside of time."

The only problem, but a terribly difficult one, is to what extent such "voluntary" or "spontaneous" work can be integrated into a technological society.

P. You told us that we might ask indiscreet questions. Would it be too indiscreet to ask you to what tradition and to what teachers you feel the closest ties, and by which you have been the most deeply influenced?

M.E. I consider myself deeply influenced, I can almost say "formed," or "shaped," by the Indian tradition. I had the great opportunity to live and learn in India as a young man, being twenty-one years old when I arrived in Poonamalee and almost twenty-five when I left Calcutta. Thanks to my Indian experience, I discovered my own Eastern Orthodox tradition, and I learned how to approach and understand other religious creations.

My teacher at the University of Calcutta was Surendranath Dasgupta, the author of the great five-volume *History of Indian Philosophy*. He guided me in the fascinating intricacies of Panini's Sanskrit grammar, and helped me to translate almost *in extenso* the three famous commentaries of the *Yoga Sūtra*. In 1930–31, I spent six months at the Himalayan *ashram* at Rishikesh, where I had the chance to practice Yoga under the guidance of Swami Shivananda, who completed his first book in that winter of 1931. (In the twenty-five years that followed, he wrote more than two hundred volumes). But the simple fact of living among Indians—in Dasgupta's house in Bhovanipore, in Shantiniketan, in Benares, and in so many villages of Bengal and Orissa—was an uninterrupted series of experiences and spiritual discoveries. It was in a poor peasant's house near Chandernagore that I understood the function of *icons* and I realized how misleading such terms as "idols" and "idolatrous" can be.

P. Do you believe that for a serious search it is necessary to find a teacher? And if so, how can a would-be disciple distinguish the true from the false? Are there signs of the genuine master, like the signs of the Buddha?

M.E. The teacher is indispensable. Anyone who *really* wants to find a teacher will find him. Of course, I do not have in mind the innumerable self-proclaimed "teachers," "*gurus*," or "initiates" who have become so popular in recent years. A *real* teacher is not necessarily well known.

2

◆

An Interview with Joseph Campbell by Michael McKnight

"The Old Ones," VOL. 5:1, February, 1980

Elders and Guides

Professor Joseph Campbell is past eighty, as he tells everyone, and indeed has to tell us or we would never know it. His vigor, wit, and youthful appearance are such that the usual reaction to this statement is disbelief, then astonishment. But longevity apart, Joseph Campbell's enormous work and international reputation in the field of mythology (which might well have remained a remote, mysterious Never-Never Land in our century without his explorations) warrant him the respectful and affectionate title of "The Grand Old Man of Myth." In the following conversation he talks with Michael McKnight, then director of a Mythology Program at the University of Vermont, about the idea of age as teacher, focusing on the life and work of the great German Heinrich Zimmer, guide and elder to the young Campbell.

If Campbell had not undertaken the arduous task of editing and translating Zimmer's lectures and notes after Zimmer's sudden death 1943, it is improbable that the German scholar's works would be known outside of a small circle of scholars. For twelve years Campbell labored over this material, and from this extraordinary effort emerged the four monumental volumes in the Bollingen series: Myths and Symbols in Indian Art and Civilization (1946), The King and the Corpse (1948), Philosophies of India (1951), and The Art of Indian Asia. His reminiscences of Zimmer warmly suggest the chain of transmission and some new ways of looking at the older generation.

MICHAEL McKNIGHT In the course of talking with Zimmer's widow, Christiane, she mentioned that when Zimmer came to this country the first thing he bought was a pair of blue jeans and a flannel shirt because he thought this was the greatest—not "hippy" clothes exactly, but something like that.

JOSEPH CAMPBELL Oh yes, he moved right over. He changed his name to Henry R. Zimmer—Americanized his name. In fact his book on medicine was published by Johns Hopkins under "Henry R. Zimmer."

M.M. Before coming here, I know he established a long-standing relationship with Carl Jung. . . .

J.C. Yes, you know Jung edited his work on Sri Ramana Maharshi, *Der Weg zum Selbst*. I think they met at the first Eranos meeting in 1933. Zimmer's *Kunstform und Yoga** caught Jung's fancy and introduced the whole mystery of the mandala to Jung. At least, I'm pretty sure that was where Jung got it.

For the first Eranos meeting, Zimmer was invited. Some people who had been there told me they were like a pair of bodhisattvas—laughing and enjoying each other. Zimmer was there for three or four of those sessions. Then he came over here, and that ended that. It was one of those *Wahlverwandtschaften* things, where the two people who meet are just made to enjoy each other.

M.M. It seems as if there was some kind of exchange, some kind of transmission of wisdom going on there. When you and Zimmer came together—and I realize it was a kind of chance meeting—this seemed to happen again. Certainly without your meeting, his name wouldn't be as familiar as it is. Who else would have taken on the "translation" of his work?

J.C. Nobody I can think of.

M.M. Do you feel then that you were completing his vocation as an interpreter of Eastern thought to the West?

*Artistic Form and Yoga in the Sacred Art of India by H.R. Zimmer. Translated by Gerald Chapple and James B. Lawson in collaboration with J. Michael McKnight, Princeton University Press, 1984.

J.C. I felt more that I was starting my own vocation! Zimmer was the first person I ever heard speak about myths who spoke about them the way I was thinking about them—that is to say, not as items for a curiosity cabinet, but as guides. He was the first I ever heard speak that way! I had already discovered Coomaraswamy's writings. In fact, I had known Coomaraswamy's work for some four or five years before I met Zimmer. When I did meet him I had already started *The Hero with a Thousand Faces*, and was working on *The Skeleton Key to Finnegans Wake*, so I was way into that world. Hearing Zimmer's lectures and the way in which these myths came out, not as curiosities over there somewhere, but as *models* for understanding your own life—this is what I had felt myths to be all this time. Of course, Jung had it, but not just the way Zimmer did. I never knew anyone who had such a gift for interpreting a symbolic image. You'd sit down at the table with him and bring up something—he'd talk about the symbolism of onion soup. I heard him do it! I don't remember what it was, but he went off on onion soup . . . oh God! This was a genius!

M.M. One question that I have is how he came to be such an interpreter of myth and symbol. I read his own biographical sketch, and it seemed that he didn't ever feel the answer was to be found in the European tradition.

J.C. No, he didn't. I'll tell you what he told me. His father was one of the great Celtic scholars of all time . . .

M.M. Yes, he calls him "a titan."

J.C. And Zimmer was brought up in a world of major scholarship—I mean that late nineteenth-century German scholarship that has not been equaled. It's basic to the whole thing—I don't care what subject you're interested in—those are the men who *did* it! They were the first professional scholars in the world. The Germans looked the field over, asked: what's to be done? and went in and did it. This is what hit me when I was a student in France. I went over there to study medieval French, old French of Provençal. Basic works? In German! So, the first thing I thought was: I can't speak or read German, so what the hell am I doing here in France when the things I *have* to know how to read are in German! The next year I went to Germany, and then the world broke wide open for me.

Now Zimmer, with his father's impulse, was working in that area, in

Indo-European philology; then he had a year of military duty. The day he was to be dismissed, the trumpet blows for the First World War. So, he was five years in the military life. Comes out: Iron Cross with Palms. Christiane may have told you what it was he did in the war, but I think he was in the Intelligence, and since he knew Sanskrit, he related to the Indian captives. He was working with some of them, the prisoners of war, and two thoughts came into his head: first, he thought of the Indian philosophy as a complement to what we had here. Second, he determined that he would not translate anything that he didn't think he understood. You know those translations of oriental texts where the translator says of the passage on which he is working: "But this is absurd!" Well, Zimmer decided to know what the thing was before he produced a translation. Then, just at that time when he was mustered out of the army, Sir John Woodroffe's tantric texts were being published. These were the first well-edited publications of the tantric texts, and Zimmer told me: "I drank those in as a baby drinks in milk." You know that kind of reading experience yourself, where you hit it, and you're building your own insides by pulling this stuff into you—that's the way he worked. And also, he had an inherent talent for amplifying the imagery through his own experience.

I learned this from him, that one should not be afraid of one's own interpretation of a symbol. It will come to you as a message, and will open out. The key to this is in that little preface that I built out of some scraps of his writing, "The Dilettante Among Symbols" at the opening of *The King and the Corpse. That's* Zimmer! When an image had opened to him that way (and mind you, he knew one hell of a lot about symbols), he'd know just where to turn to validate his own interpretation of the experience of it. He would check it. But his interpretation of symbols always came out of him personally, reinforced by a host of clues from the East.

M.M. And with a sense of delight. . . .

J.C. Yes, that *delecto* . . . he had delight! I'll not forget some of those lectures! He was just bubbling over! And he could play it—this way or that way or throw it around. It wasn't just bumm, bumm, bumm, down the line.

M.M. Christiane was originally his student—and she mentioned that he had an extraordinary teaching style, that even with Sanskrit grammar, he was very enthusiastic and almost inspired.

J.C. He made you feel that you understood Sanskrit. Anyone studying Sanskrit with Zimmer would have learned it in a couple of months, at least how to read the epic Sanskrit which is relatively easy. The Kavya poetry—that would be something else again. But the *Mahabharata*, the *Ramayana*—you'd be reading them in a couple of months. He was wonderful.

But that wasn't what I sat in on. I was already well along in my own teaching career when he came over. I was helping Swami Nikhilananda with *The Gospel of Sri Ramakrishna*, and I knew people in the Jung Foundation. They all knew of Zimmer's arrival here. I had never heard of Zimmer. I met him first at one of the evenings that Swami Nikhilananda liked to put on where he'd invite people and prepare a curry dinner for them. (He was a really good cook.) Then I learned almost immediately that Zimmer was about to deliver some lectures at Columbia. It was not Columbia who had invited him to give the lectures. It was the *Jungfrauen*, the ladies of the Jung Foundation who had discovered a room on the campus where he could lecture. It was at the top of Low Library—a little museum up there. I heard that he was going to be lecturing, and having met him at Nikhilananda's, I was eager to hear him. He was a lovely presence. There was such a stream of marvelous wisdom pouring from him!

There were three people inscribed for his lectures, plus Marguerite Bloch, the lady who was the director of the museum: namely me, a woman from the Jung Foundation, and a Polish sculptress who emanated a perfume that almost set everybody crazy. Well, Zimmer lectured as though he were lecturing to an auditorium! He was not a good lecturer in English yet; he couldn't do it right off the top of his head, so he had written out his lectures. I have them all in my files—the ones I turned into those books—on little pieces of paper about six by four inches. And he would type out the lines—not in a running prose, but in stroke phrases. And he would underline in red the syllable to be accented in each word. He *worked* on those lectures, and they were great. And every now and then when he'd come to the point of telling a story, he'd put the thing down and tell you the myth—always with a wonderful sense of the humor that is the life of myth. Well, those were stunning lectures and those are the ones I made into the great big two-volume work, *The Art of Indian Asia*. That was the first semester.

The second semester, he had to move into another room, because there were about fifty people this time. My father had a saying: you can't hide a good restaurant, and Columbia couldn't hide Zimmer. In the fall, he started a series of lectures—then in one week, he died. He gave a lecture one Friday night; he was breathing somewhat heavily; he went home. Christiane phoned me the next morning and said he was very sick and she was afraid. I was amazed. And we were burying him the next week . . . it was like that.

M.M. It was pneumonia, wasn't it?

J.C. Yes, it was pneumonia that had not been properly diagnosed; he'd been walking around with it for a couple of weeks. He was a big strong man; he just thought he had a cold or something like that, and, zing, it took him away.

Well, that was a stunner! But then Christiane asked me if I'd edit this material—his American lectures—and I thought: a couple of years.

It was twelve years I worked on those notes.

His first series of lectures was the set that I turned into *The Art of Indian Asia*, which was the last book on which I worked. His second series was a full semester of philosophy; then came the series that I published under the title *Myths and Symbols in Indian Art and Civilization*. That was the first that I brought out. Then I did *The King and the Corpse*, which is based on written material that he had published plus the first chapter of his unfinished translation into German of the *Kalikapurana*. But the fourth semester of his teaching was the one broken off by his death. It was again a semester on philosophy, so when I started on the philosophy volume I had only a semester and a quarter of his lectures, and that was not the whole story. I found a lot more material in his notes. I phoned Jack Barrett at Bollingen, and said: Look, if you'll give me another two or three years on this book, we can have a killer here. And it is. *The Philosophies of India* is a corker!

There were some very interesting things that happened to me in the course of doing those books. Zimmer used to give his manuscripts to his friends and students just to have them read them over and help him straighten out his prose. So when I would come to certain chapters, there would be a gap. Some little lady would have kept them somewhere in her memory chest. But he had such a striking and forceful presence in his presentation that in my memory I could hear him. I would get to the point where pages were missing and a break came; I'd jump the break and pick up again where the thing resumed and do a few paragraphs of that. Then I'd see what the gap was between the two and what had to be covered. I had talked with Zimmer a lot about these things and I would bridge the gap with four or five questions; I'd ask a question and listen, then he would dictate. The style was his style, more or less. Then when I got into doing the big book on *The Art of Indian Asia*, I could no longer hear him dictating—that was eleven or twelve years later—and I was finished. There was no way to go on.

M.M. Would you have a visual impression of him?

J.C. No, I'd just sit down and listen. There'd be a vague sense of his weight, and I'd take dictation.

M.M. Do you feel then in a sense that he was actually speaking through you somehow?

J.C. No, those were just bridges, you know; I don't have any sense of that kind of spooky thing. It was my recollection of his manner, of what he had been saying, that is what I'd hear him say—maybe I had a couple of notes of my own from the lecture. My technique handling Zimmer's material was to keep his page at my left hand and write with my right (I don't use a typewriter when I write). I was using his phrases as far as possible with a correction of some of the verbal choices, and I would try to get that baroque rhythm that he had. I would mark off with a red line whatever I had used, and sometimes I'd jump from the top to the bottom of the page and come back to the middle and so forth. It was all built out of his words and put together with a more naturally English tone and type of prose. I don't know where Zimmer ends and I begin. It was a great inspiration to me—working on that wave of his vitality.

Often when I talked with him, he had Wagner going full blast on the record player. Wagner full blast and Zimmer full blast and I'd stand there and I'd know: the whole answer to the universe is coming at me right now and I wonder if I'm understanding it or getting any particle of it! Some of those moments were really fantastic.

M.M. But you did get it; that's the marvelous thing.

J.C. Well, yes, I got it, but as I said, I worked twelve years on it.

M.M. But it was like a labor of love. . . .

J.C. It was a labor of delight! Every bit of it. It was hellish hard work, but a real, real delight.

Sometimes I wished he'd written the damn paragraph in German—the English was *just* off. That's the hardest kind of thing to get back on the track with—where it isn't *quite* correct. Also, with his enormous philological knowledge he could make up words! He would put in a word that he thought ought to be an English one, and there wouldn't be anything in English quite like it.

I wouldn't have been able to do the books at all if I hadn't known that Zimmer would have liked the way I was doing it. He was extremely amusing with relation to what we call academic formalities.

There was one chapter on *Satyagraha*—the Gandhi piece which I wrote from my notes of his lecture and what I remembered—that somebody had run off with. When I was in Calcutta, they gave me the newspaper one day, and here in a framed box on the front page was some Indian declaring that the Westerner, the white man, just can't understand Gandhi, and that Gandhi's message is as follows. I went on reading, and my God, I was recognizing my own prose! It was this chapter! They were pulling it right out of the book! That was very amusing, and pleasing in a way.

I had a double advantage—not only Zimmer there as a model in those years, but I was teaching young women who weren't the least bit interested in academic details. They wanted to know what a myth might mean to *them*. With this double inspiration, Zimmer and my students, I was held to the *life* of my subject, and this is the thing that built whatever it is I have had as a career, which I think has been a pretty good one.

M.M. Understanding myths and symbols tends to bring one to a perspective; at least it's hopeful. Even in bad situations, you can see the thread.

J.C. Absolutely! The bad situation is one of the disintegrating moments in myth out of which integration comes. And what is it that's collapsing? And why? Because something was missing. It's collapsing because it was off balance. Well, let that go and find the opposite. That's what Zimmer did with the War. He went to India.

M.M. But he didn't go there physically.

J.C. He never saw India!

M.M. He says in the biographical sketch that he reached a point where he realized he couldn't get any more out of texts. He had studied them all. And he realized that the real teacher was experience—it was life itself. That recognition seems to have elevated him from an ordinary teacher to an extraordinary teacher.

J.C. It's hard for me to think now that he was in his fifties when he died, and a man now in his fifties could be my son. Still, he's in my mind as the elder, the guide. I've studied with a lot of special people. I've had very, very wonderful luck in the people who became my (what they now call) gurus—even from the time I was a little boy. It was never really a "guru"—nobody ever took charge of me the way a guru does—but there were people who were my inspirations. And Zimmer was the last one.

M.M. There hasn't been one since?

J.C. No, not of that type.

M.M. How many were there before?

J.C. Oh, there was a long line. From the time I was a little boy, the people in school with whom I was working, then in college, graduate school, and then in my off-campus life as well. I've always had inspired connections with the really wonderful, wonderful teachers—some of them not "teachers," just men that I admired and talked to. But Zimmer topped it off.

3

◆

An Interview with Adin Steinsaltz
by William and Louise Welch

"Hierarchy," VOL. IX:1, January, 1984

Becoming Unstable: Hierarchy and Evolution

*R*abbi *Adin Steinsaltz, Director of the Shefa Institute and head of the Israel Institute for Talmudic Publications in Jerusalem, is a scholar, linguist, teacher, scientist, writer, artist, and social critic. His achievements include an ongoing translation into modern Hebrew of the Babylonian Talmud, and treatises on such disparate subjects as French literature, science fiction, archeology, mysticism, Israeli politics, and zoology. In spite of his formidable learning in so many fields, his way of speaking and writing remains accessible in any of the various languages in which he is fluent. Delighted audiences of his lectures here, as well as readers of* The Thirteen-Petalled Rose *(Basic Books, Inc., 1980), can attest to the humor and charm with which he conveys an illuminating thought.*

Dr. William J. Welch, a former president of the American Heart Association, has retired from a distinguished medical career and is now free to pursue full-time his other lifelong interests in traditional and religious ideas and practice. His inner and outer journeys in these fields are actively shared by his wife, Louise Welch. Both are writers; besides reviews and articles in various publications, What Happened in Between, *by William Welch, was published by Braziller in 1972, and* Orage with Gurdjieff in America *by Louise Welch, by Routledge & Kegan Paul in 1982.*

On a recent visit to Israel, the Welches met, conversed with, and were deeply impressed by, Rabbi Steinsaltz. They write: "When the opportunity came our way, we were grateful to turn for light on this troublesome subject of hierarchy to a man widely schooled at the interface between reason and revelation. Rabbi Steinsaltz received us kindly in Jerusalem in the fall of 1982, and when he was in New York the following spring, he consented to be interviewed. We soon realized why his evening seminars in Jerusalem attract devoted students, scholars, and notables from around the world."

◆

WILLIAM WELCH We live in an egalitarian moment in which it is considered that everyone is equal and everyone is free, and the idea of hierarchy is perceived as an arbitrary imposition on the freedom of man. I wonder how realistic this conception is from your point of view.

ADIN STEINSALTZ My point of view is almost the opposite. Egalitarian ideas are not supported by any evidence. The inequality of man is blatantly apparent. The only way we can find any support for the idea of equality is in a very difficult religious concept: the concept that people are born in the image of the Lord and are therefore equal. There is no other argument that I have heard that serves any purpose. All egalitarian movements are an outcome of Judeo-Christian ideas that contain within them the notion of receiving a divine soul that for everyone is more or less the same. We can speak—in a way—of the equality of souls mostly because we can't see them! But it is very hard to speak about equality in any other way. All forces everywhere, within and without, work against equality. People are so inherently different—not only different, but unequal—that it requires a constant struggle to accept the notion of some kind of equality. The only justification for the idea is what you may call a mystical one: even though people don't appear to be equal, there is something equal in them.

From this point of view, whether it is a good thing or not such a good thing, hierarchy seems to me to be a given element; inherent in creation and nature. This is nature—everything else is an attempt to change nature.

W.W. The evidence of hierarchy in the physiological organization of man is quite clear; from above downward, with semi-independent functions, each with a certain autonomy but subject to control from above. Might there be a relationship between the higher and lower in our psyche and some corresponding potential, if not actual, authority?

A.S. The physiological model has the advantage of stressing that the hierarchical involves interdependence. For instance, the mind is far superior to the legs—anyone would prefer to have his leg cut off rather than to have his head cut off. On the other hand, there are functions that the legs perform which the head cannot. Recently I taught some ancient texts about inner spiritual hierarchy—for hierarchy exists not only as an outer biological and social structure, but also as an inner one. There are higher and lower forces within our world, within our souls, and within our concepts. And even there, hierarchy is interdependent. There are lower elements—clearly lower by every definition—that have a basic power which makes them not only worthwhile, but in certain situations far more important than higher ones.

There are many discussions in Jewish mystical tradition about interrelationships between mind, or intellect, and emotion. In our view, in the hierarchy of the soul emotions are below mind, because mind gives meaning and direction to emotions. The powers of conceptualization and of thinking are called the father and mother; the emotions are called the children. It is a common way of describing them; but even so, we know that in the working of the soul there are instances when the mind cannot do anything. The intellect is powerless to achieve things. That which emotions can achieve, the mind cannot, but the emotions cannot operate without some kind of subject-object relationship. Emotions, dependent on information and direction supplied by the mind, can only work within that context. The mind works as a watcher, or censor, of things without and within.

It has often been noted that the strength of emotional and intellectual ties is very unequal. Whether we like it or not, emotionally we get attached to things and aren't able to change our attachment with the intellect.

LOUISE WELCH Where do you place the sense of values? I think different levels exist in what we value, and how we value it.

A.S. We consider the sense of values as something that comes before, or hierarchically above, conscious mind. We believe there are powers within every framework that give direction. I am speaking now not about mystical experiences but in a practical context: on one level my mind is made up about whether it wants to be for or against something. Then it creates the network and the building blocks for my basic attitude. Later, some kind of appropriate emotion arises. Because emotion is secondary, in order to develop it needs something to build upon. If I don't have any picture of whatever it is, I cannot have any emotion—love or hatred—

L.W. Or reverence.

A.S. Or even reverence. I have to have a point of view; and to have a feeling of awe, of facing the unknown, on an emotional basis, one has to have a very deep intellectual background. In the Middle Ages people said

that the peak of knowledge is "I don't know." The question is: if that is so, what is the difference between the person who has no knowledge whatever and the person who knows? The difference is that the person who knows, knows that he doesn't know. The person who does not know, doesn't even have knowledge of his ignorance. So the feeling of reverence is enhanced by knowing the distance. Even if I think that something is far beyond me, I need to know the gap in order to have the feeling of reverence and awe. If I don't know about the gap, the distance doesn't make any sense to me. To know that I don't know is more than just making a statement; to be emotionally involved in it, I have to have an idea of what the meaning of it is. Newton supposedly said that he felt like a small child playing with pebbles on the shore of the sea of knowledge—to feel that really and truly, you have to know as much as Newton did. Those who don't know may say it, but they don't feel it emotionally.

Emotional life is hierarchically dependent on conceptual life; conceptual life makes it possible to have emotional life. And conceptual life is hierarchically below a value system that makes things desirable or nondesirable. I have given lectures concerning what philosophers say about the nature of proof. Philosophy has no real way of defining proof, except what is said by some conservative philosophers: that the proof that something is true is that it clicks. That is the only way I know that something is true, that I have proved it: there is some kind of click. That is possibly the highest hierarchy in our conscious minds—that which says one relationship is true, and another is not. So we are, in fact, judging things, and we say: that fits and that doesn't fit. Now, we cannot explain the way something fits together, because explanation itself comes back to the same question: does it click? If it does, the explanation makes sense. The nature of proof is something that, within the soul, is above anything in the conscious mind—even above the power of pure reason. Above pure reason stands something—we don't know what it is—but it convinces us that something *is*.

L.W. Is the vision of hierarchy essential, then, for the movement upwards of the sense of values, and the spiritual search?

A.S. There is something that has to be achieved. If there is no hierarchy, nothing can be achieved by moving from one point to another. When there is a difference, movement makes sense; when there is no difference movement does not make sense. If one goes into it further, one gets into very complex concepts of movement and what movement means; we would be speaking about the theory of relativity. In the abstract, when there is no interrelation, movement or size doesn't make any sense. Without a scale, there is no movement; to advance or retreat depends on having a direction—a beginning and an end.

L.W. One has the sense that along with the force of emotion, and the polarity of like and dislike, there can be at times an intelligence of feeling that has its own quality. You place the mind above emotion, but where do you place this intelligence of the emotions?

A.S. People say that the heart has its own reason. We believe that every emotion is made, roughly speaking, of three parts, as mind is made up of the same three parts. There is the intelligence of the emotion; the emotions of the emotion; and the mechanics of emotion, getting it expressed. So the intelligence, or mind of the emotion, does exist. We believe that the intellectual powers are also made like this. There is intellectual thought and emotional thought, because intellect has in it an emotional part. That is one reason why the process of thinking sometimes becomes enjoyable per se; intelligence is not pure, it also has an emotional part. The reason of the emotion works in a different way, on a different level; that is the inner hierarchy. Emotion has its own way of conceptualizing, not intellectually but by creating images.

W.W. Is there a concept in Judaism that this model within the individual is a reflection of an order which exists on another level? Do the same elements exist on a cosmic scale?

A.S. Given the creation by God of a complete universe, it is a basic assumption that everything is interconnected. One can see something like that by looking at drops of water; one sees reflections, smaller ones and bigger ones, like in a house of mirrors; the same thing, the same nature, reflected in different ways. It follows that if I would know perfectly, completely, entirely, one part, then I would know the whole.

It is a beautiful thing: when God says, "Let us make man," He is calling the whole universe—"Let *us* make man." And each contributes something: the foxes and the lions, the monkeys and the angels all give something! So we are the result of everything that is. The idea is that we contain (and this point is considered essential) the mind-body point of connection; the same hierarchy that exists in the body exists in the mind.

One of the ways to explain the basic concept of our religion is to say that because we are human beings, we have to correct; we have the ability to repair. Because we have free will, we are also the only ones who have the ability to distort. One of our problems is that of choice. There is an attempt to become better; it is like making corrections for a lens. The lens became for some reason not right, so it distorts whatever is seen through it. We believe the main duty, the chief work of human beings, is to make corrections until it is possible to transmit the right picture.

L.W. The question in my mind, before you said that, is that there is an order evident in our bodies and in all nature; everything is perfect—except me. If I am a reflection of this perfect order, why am I not perfect?

A.S. Free will is an element of disorder. It is also the only element of advancement.

Any kind of movement is a way of destroying a system of order. Walking, for example, is *becoming unstable*. Running is becoming even more unstable. Flying in a plane creates a different kind of instability; the plane becomes less and less stable until it takes off, and then it restabilizes and gains equilibrium. Movement destroys equilibrium all the time; the power to move is also the power to destroy order. The imperfection is inherent, because I am the only creature that has independent volition, and the only creature in the universe that can distort. These distortions are part of our common human work for coming to a higher point, because other creatures, seemingly, cannot move of their own volition, and we can. And being able to move means that we can move in different directions. We don't have the same biological point of view as other creatures; we are free of instinct—not entirely, but to a very great degree. That is our power, and that is our downfall.

W.W. You almost say *choice*, don't you?

A.S. Yes, I am always saying *choice*. Animals and plants don't have that element of choice. It used to be a habit of mind, when I felt angry or discontented, to go to the zoo and watch the animals; animals have a certain type of perfection that we don't. In a way, it's the same thing that makes babies beautiful. Sometimes you wonder why so many babies are born wise and beautiful, and why when they become adults, they lose both those qualities! It is because babies are innocent; they reflect the power of relation and choice. They reflect something which we call the great order of things. The bigger they become, the more they are able to move. There are some people who, as they grow older, clearly become wiser—not just more knowledgeable; there is a great difference between the two—and also more beautiful. Their choice, their achievement of consciousness, is a growing from one set of relationships to another, a bigger one, a better one. On the other hand, there are some people who make the choice of distorting, and they become less wise and less beautiful—everything less. So as I say, this difficulty of mankind, being the one creature that is not in order, is our strength and our weakness.

L.W. You are speaking of levels of order, aren't you? Because doesn't a human being then choose to live according to another, higher order?

A.S. That is what I am saying. We are in movement. In every set of circumstances, every level of hierarchy, there is stability of some kind. Movement is a disturbing element, and also rather dangerous. Between one step of a ladder and another, there is a void; the void is necessary because it makes the difference between the levels. But if I want to move from the first rung to the second or the third, I have to take the risk of passing through this void, of abolishing my foothold in one place in order to get to another, and in between I may fall down. It often happens. So our process of growing, from the physical to the spiritual, is getting from one set of ways of behavior, and so on, to a different one, which we hope is a higher one. It is not necessarily so, but it is a movement into a different order in which things, after some time, again become more or less stabilized. In any process of inner growth or evolution, there is the same problem of getting from one point to another. Being born is in a way ceasing to exist in one type of order, and entering a different type of order in which almost all the rules are changed. As a fetus, I don't breathe, and my life system is entirely different. Being born is the shock of transfer to a set of circumstances in which almost everything is done in a different way, in which there is an order of a different kind. Dying is doing the same thing—again, in a different way, perhaps coming to a point where I discard certain things about my being. The shock there is the transfer from one set of circumstances to another. Our notion of people going to hell has to do with this transfer. I might be magnificently suited to survive in this world, but now I have to go into another world with other rules. If a person doesn't grow through adaptation to a certain order and then moves into another one, he is unable to deal with it. It is like the tadpole and the frog. We see this all the time: men who were wonderful as boys in school are not necessarily wonderful as adults out of school. Because a change creates a necessity for a different order.

W.W. The transformation of a tadpole to a frog, or from one set of

conditions in life to another in death, is something that happens automatically; but isn't there another possibility of transformation for human beings, an intentional one?

A.S. Oh, that is what it *should* be! That is what I meant about a person going to heaven or hell; the process of learning, of education, determines which way one takes. The tadpole doesn't learn to become a frog; but for man, as we know, it is very hard work.

As a human being, I have some ability to change consciously to a different order, but actually, we set our hearts on a certain place and don't want to get any higher. There is an old Russian story about a simple soldier who rescued the Czar from some danger. The Czar told him he could ask for whatever he wanted, and the soldier said, "Please, change my commanding officer!" Instead of moving upward in the hierarchy, I just want to shift into a more comfortable position on the same level.

I would say that hierarchy is an infinite number of orders of laws, one above the other. Each order has within it an inner order; and with this interdependence, there is a context in which we are all equal, in which all existence is equal in this eternal interdependence.

w.w. Are you saying that authority is determined by the degree of consciousness?

A.S. I am a part of something. Authority is the rule of the higher over the lower. I think that, as you say, possibly hierarchy is defined by greater consciousness. Julian Huxley seems an unlikely source to quote, but in speaking about evolution he says that only in this sense of growing consciousness can we make sense of evolution as a progressive line. Advance is not in terms of "fitness"; if evolution is simply a matter of the survival of the fittest, it would have stopped with the cockroach. But there is a different striving, a striving for more consciousness; and in this way we may say we have something above the cockroach.

So power or authority is connected with the level of consciousness, in every level, in every degree. It determines what is bigger, what is smaller; the bigger is bigger because it can encompass the smaller. In every hierarchy the one that knows where to put the others is the one who is in charge. The highest in the hierarchy is the one who can put all the parts in some kind of complete order. Otherwise, whatever the official, apparent order may be, it is a false hierarchy. In a real hierarchy, the one who is most conscious about what is happening is the higher. Other people may perhaps be more powerful, but they are not higher.

One of the things that makes life so complicated is that there is not one type of hierarchy, but many. And because there are conflicting hierarchies, we get confused. There is the hierarchy of the good, the hierarchy of the wise, the hierarchy of the powerful. Each is different. I would say that all designs somehow end up at a convergent point; but in our world they are not convergent. The problem of existence is that different hierarchies are not aligned, not compatible with each other. It has been said before that in this world we have the clever and the good—and they are usually not the same people! A world in which they would become more and more identical would be a better world.

So our problem is not lack of hierarchy, but too many hierarchies. Our problem is to make order among them, to arrange the different hierarchies in a hierarchical formation. We have different types of ladders, and when they are not arranged among themselves, they don't lead anywhere. What we need is a way of attaching the separate ladders into one which becomes far bigger. But every group has its own ladder and doesn't want to share it, and because of this we come to the point where no one in his separate way can go any higher. So we divide and come to a sort of compromise that says: because we don't agree on which is better, let us assume that nothing is better. Because we don't agree on who should be on top, nobody should be there.

w.w. What authority will we all accept?

a.s. We all accept that there is a certain ladder; what we dispute about is which one. The ladders are incompatible; they don't meet. We are dealing in different areas. The differences between us—for instance, between the believing man and the knowledgeable man—often takes precedence over something that is more urgent: which ladder is the more important one.

l.w. Is it finally a matter of agreement or decision? Or is there one which simply is more important? It seems there would have to be, if there is real hierarchy.

a.s. I would say there definitely is one; that we don't agree about it doesn't mean anything. All of us agree that what is most positive should be at the head. The question is not so much about hierarchy as about what hierarchy to adopt. Almost every religion tries to give some way of measuring things, some kind of scale. We need a way of bringing different things to some kind of common scale, some common value into which they can all be translated. That is what we are in search of.

4

◆

An Interview with Henri Tracol

"Food," VOL. IX:4, November, 1984

A Question of Balance

*F*ormer *journalist, photographer, and anthropologist with the Musée de l'Homme, Henri Tracol has been for many years one of the chief exponents of the teaching of G.I. Gurdjieff. The system taught by Gurdjieff includes within it a complex elaboration of the place of food on cosmological and psychological levels. We sought out Mr. Tracol in his summer retreat in the south of France to speak with him about these ideas in the light of his own long experience. He greeted us in his shaded courtyard where among the trees, herbs, and flowers were several of his large stone sculptures—massive forms smoothed out of a local white stone. His latest work, "Ganesha," awaited final polishing in an open-air studio adjoining the main house.*

Once inside the cool, high-ceilinged living room, we sat together at a large, old wooden table. Mr. Tracol responded to our questions with great interest and intensity. Gentle, unpretentious, incisive, full of quick humor, he seemed somehow to accompany his words. As we spoke, the exchange became not only a discussion of abstract ideas but a kind of nourishment in itself.

◆

PARABOLA We might start out by speaking about physical food. In the United States now, perhaps in Europe as well, there is a great interest in experimentation—in macrobiotics, in vegetarianism, in organically grown

41

foods, and it becomes almost a moral issue what sort of food we eat. But in the Gospels Christ says, "For what goes into your mouth, that will not defile you, but that which issues from your mouth—it is that which will defile you." Does it make a difference what sort of food we eat?

HENRI TRACOL It certainly does. Now, what is the point of view from which we could evaluate this first food, physical food? Of course, we cannot be without a certain discrimination about what is good or bad from an ordinary point of view. But what is more important? First, this question can be understood only in relationship to the whole. You have to be attentive to your food, and not only the first food, but to the others. Whether you know it or not, you depend very much on what you eat, and breathe, and so on. It is not only necessary for the physical body, but also for the whole of your being. Food is needed not just to sustain your physical existence, it's also for other purposes. It is not to be belittled. Now, of course, you can eat the best food, drink the best drinks, and if you do not understand what it is for, it is lost—very largely, lost. What is absorbed and what feeds you really is a very small proportion of what is given. A small part sustains the outer existence, but most of it is wasted. Now I think of something that has been very striking for me. Perhaps you know a book by Viktor Frankl, *Man's Search for Meaning*. He speaks about the way people who were doomed to death in concentration camps could survive. What they ate was very, very little, very insignificant. But for them there was something much more important. There was a wish to be. Even though they did not fully realize the importance of it, they perceived that something was necessary, and was far more important than their comfort, their despair, and so on. They knew that something was offered them, and they wanted to live. And on that basis, they could survive in conditions that were impossible—medically, impossible.

So this is what is really important, to understand that the question of food is not just an outer, mechanical process, it is also something of significance. Insofar as you are able to be attentive to this perspective, it is really of value that you do not treat this food as something insignificant.

I would also say, in another field, that there was something that Mr. Gurdjieff never accepted—a completely stupid disregard for the body, or any kind of scorning of the body. He evoked a respect for the body. In the same perspective, what is really important there is not only that which we ordinarily call the body, with its pleasure, or fear of pain and so on, but the body itself as a place where something can be born again, and develop. So, it has to be respected, and its needs, its real needs, met. There are many misinterpretations of what he said or wrote about the necessity to compel the body to obey higher imperatives. It is not *against* the body, it is *for* the body. And the body knows it, too!

P. Mr. Gurdjieff has written that it is necessary to strive to have everything necessary and satisfying for the physical body. This puzzles me—not only everything necessary, but also everything satisfying. When is this possible—to have both?

H.T. It implies the need for a degree of understanding. If we draw a list of what is necessary and what is satisfying it will be futile, of course.

It is a question of balance, mostly. And it means a balance with other needs as well. Otherwise, something can be quite satisfactory for the body itself, as separate from the rest; but it creates a lack of balance. What is necessary and what is really satisfactory is a balance between all the different needs of the being—physical, and psychological, and spiritual.

P. So the body needs this balance in order to be truly satisfied.

H.T. Yes.

P. How do you see the point of the dietary restrictions that occur in so many traditions—Islam, Judaism, Buddhism? So many traditions set out very clear rules about what to eat, and when, and how much. What is the point of such rules?

H.T. Mr. Gurdjieff has spoken of such rules, and of how they are always linked with other rules. It is a whole, and if something is missing in the other rules, then it is pointless. You forget what the reason is. At certain times it may be necessary to refrain from certain foods, and at other times not. In any case it is not the real point. We have to adapt ourselves to conditions—to outer conditions, of course—but to inner conditions as well. Otherwise we make fools of ourselves trying to stick to something as though it had to be followed at any cost.

P. Did Mr. Gurdjieff subscribe to any particular rules about eating?

H.T. In *Meetings with Remarkable Men* he speaks of his encounter with an old Persian dervish at a time when, as a young man, he was very keen to follow certain rules; for example, in regard to the thorough chewing of food. Asked by the dervish why he was so scrupulously practicing such a demanding method of eating, the young Gurdjieff explained at length why this was highly recommended by certain schools of Indian yogis. To which the old man shook his head and said, "Let God kill him who does not know and yet presumes to show others the way to the doors of His Kingdom." After explaining to his young visitor that it was imperative, at his age, not to deprive his stomach of the opportunity to exercise itself in its natural work, the old man concluded by hinting that those who recommended such mastication had, as is said, "heard a bell without knowing where the sound came from."

As a matter of fact, Mr. Gurdjieff trained us to eat all sorts of things that were not particularly recommended! He would insist that you at times had to eat all sorts of greasy, fatty foods, all sorts of ingredients that would be very, very hot—which from an ordinary medical point of view were impossible to accept. Of course there were those who needed to be on a special diet and he was resilient enough to exempt them. But otherwise, you *had* to eat what was served. He would go to the market and choose the ingredients and would be preparing the food from early in the morning for the evening. He would allow very few to help him. He had his own ways. And when people were eating with him, he was very attentive to the way you took in food. It was very important for him. When he saw someone who was absorbed in a question he perhaps wanted to ask and was eating without knowing he was eating, he would frown, and sometimes scold and so on. So there was a respect for food that was necessary. No matter *what* it was!

P. This respect for food that you mention seems to have almost completely disappeared from our lives—perhaps because most of us are so far away from the growing and raising of food, we no longer know what it has to cost for it to be available to us.

H.T. It is true, it is not easy to obtain. But, you see, when we speak of food, we speak of one category, forgetting or neglecting the others, and I think it's misleading. In fact, there are all sorts of food, and it is a question of the whole being. There is the idea that there are three kinds of food: ordinary food, air, and impressions. You can go on existing for days without ordinary food. You can survive if you do not breathe for a few minutes perhaps, not very long. But you cannot exist one second without impressions. This idea is fantastic. One can hear it, perhaps be surprised, and say, "That's very interesting." But it's forgotten immediately, because it is not properly received. Perhaps it demands a lifetime to understand what it means. The food of impressions is taken in constantly. You need this third kind of food in order to really take in the first food. In order to breathe, you need it too. What is essential there is most neglected, ignored—it is fantasy for us. Of course it is closely related to another idea which very largely escapes us, and which is that only higher centers can really receive, properly, the food of impressions. Higher centers—and it is said that higher centers are fully developed in a human being. They function perfectly well. What is missing is the proper link with lower centers. In *Beelzebub*, Mr. Gurdjieff speaks of what happens to this finer food of impressions. Most of it is lost. But part of it is always maintained and perceived and absorbed for the development of higher components of a being. So, without our knowing—and especially when we are asleep— something is taking place there.

P. These impressions are being received all the time, so it is a question of digestion?

H.T. Yes; in fact something is digested without our knowing it. Regard- less of what becomes of our lower centers—the higher centers need to go on existing. It is said also that accidentally—but it is not mere accident, it is for a higher purpose—we receive the necessary help for the digestion of these finer impressions. Of course I do not claim to understand this, but it does evoke something in me. So we are made use of for the sake of the higher centers, and even though we seem to be cut from them, they are there.

P. It really does seem as though it is impossible to speak of one food at a time, as though we eat at one moment, and breathe at another and then receive an impression.

H.T. We are enslaved by the notion of time, of course.

These questions also evoke the mystery of what is called conscious attention. Ordinarily speaking, what we call conscious attention is when we translate our experience immediately into our ordinary terms. "This is that": we define. But in fact this sort of attention is just on the border— it is superficial. It is an automatism that goes on and on, and the machine is very good. It works very well, outerly. But for the whole of the being, including the higher parts, it is almost insignificant—it deals with the outer part of our existence, that's all. For what is essential is not there. That's why it's so important to take into account what happens in very special conditions, as in the case of the prisoners Frankl speaks of. Ordinary conditions of existence are important, of course, they have to be taken into account. But the real meaning is not there.

P. It has been said that every creature is designed for a certain kind of food, and can be defined in relationship to what it eats. Each creature can be seen as a kind of specialist in eating certain foods. It seems that there might be here a kind of definition of the difference between human beings and all other beings in this question of impressions. Are there certain kinds of impressions that only human beings can receive? Are we sort of specialists in the possibility of receiving a certain kind of food?

H.T. Undoubtedly. Now is it for our ordinary mind to try to understand what that means? It is very dangerous, because most of the time we will translate it into terms that do not correspond. Ordinary thinking cannot cover this at all. Now, is there something that we could call higher mind? Do we know it, or do we just project an image? Is it once again a wrong work of our lower mind? It tries to define what it should be, and so on. No; I think we need to keep a kind of respect for what is given us at certain moments to perceive—not as a result of any mental combination, but something that is offered, and offered, and offered, and *for once* we perceive it. Does this perception depend on me or is this something which is granted me? I think even when it depends partly on me, it's mostly granted; and it has to be perceived as granted.

P. Several times now you have said that our energy from all sorts of food is mostly wasted. Is anything actually wasted?

H.T. One cannot help thinking of so much waste in nature. All the seeds which seem completely lost—but they are not lost; they serve for something, so nothing is lost, or wasted completely. But we cannot remain indifferent when we see what is *partly* wasted. What can be planted and can grow into a splendid tree—we are sensitive to the difference. It calls something in us. Something is there which could be fully developed—this evokes our real interest. And it applies to man as well. Of course he could be a very splendid animal for the Olympic Games, or a fantastic artist. But something is missed for the full stature of a being—I will not say one who could do everything, that is not the case; I mean one has been born with a certain balance of capacities which go far beyond what our ordinary imagination could conceive. But there is first of all a sense of balance, of right balance, and there is a certain balance in a moment when a man awakes to his own destiny. He is able to join with what is in him, what is there as a seed in him, and find the corresponding attitude and functioning which bear witness to the presence of this hidden capacity. It may not be corresponding to what could perhaps be expected from someone else, but it corresponds to what *he* is. I think this is a real source of commitment. I mean, not to dream of fantastic realization, but to be sensitive to the presence of the call of capacities which are there waiting for recognition, and waiting for completion.

P. Whatever awareness is (again a word probably misunderstood), it seems that one can sense that the quality of physical food and air and impressions would all change if there was a light of awareness on the process instead of it taking place in the dark, separated somehow. This was what Mr. Gurdjieff seemed to be calling for all the time.

H.T. Oh, yes. He knew that what was usually meant there was most of the time a far distant approach—something that did not correspond really to what he was evoking. If you are not one, whole, there is always something missing. Now a person who dreams of understanding the whole makes a fool of himself—it is simply impossible. He's just dreaming. What you can try is to open to what corresponds to you, and to you only. In a way—this is, I would say, a joke—you can understand something that God cannot understand. God cannot reduce himself to become so little! The sense of specificity, of what is possible for a particular person, evokes a completely different interest from a pretense to understand more and more and more, up to the whole. It is simply stupid. It is not what is demanded. What is offered, and demanded, is to approach what corresponds to you— and to no one else. It means also that you have to share with others—there are many things to share with others. But there is something specific to you and to no one else on the earth. In centuries and centuries you are the only one who can understand in that way, that very particular and specific way. And this is really appealing. It helps to understand that something is demanded of me.

P. Mr. Gurdjieff speaks of self-remembering very much. In reference to an earlier question, is the impression of oneself unique to human beings? Does it constitute a kind of food only humans can receive?

H.T. Another mystery. Self-remembering . . . to awake. If we begin to think in our ordinary terms, what does it mean to awake? Do I decide at a certain time to awake? And who decides? There is no answer there, except to realize that I am awakened by something. It is not that I decide to awaken and I awake; that is simply impossible. But maybe "I," with another meaning, the real "I," reminds me, calls me back. The sense of my being: it is not something that I invent, or that I think of. It is there. And it calls me back. That's self-remembering. And on this basis, there is a certain kind of awareness which comes to me. Most of the time it's enjoyed by a part which pretends to be the owner—"Oh yes, I think that." That's a betrayal. I have been given to see something, to understand something, and I try to join with it. But if I let in this pretense to be the *one who* . . . it's spoiled. Does it mean that I have to keep passive about it? Not at all. In order to keep awake, something is demanded of me. It is demanded of the whole of me, all my faculties and capacities, including my ordinary attention, my possibilities to establish connections, associations, useful associations. On behalf of what has been given me, I do not allow myself to be passive. There is something behind. Something—there is no question of reaching for anything. It is not to be reached; it is there. It conveys an objective meaning to my attempt at joining with what is offered me. If I keep that, if my ordinary, my outer self keeps that, is faithful to this recognition, then it's given me over and over again to discover what is proposed and proposed and proposed. Of course, it cannot last very long: but for a time it can last. I can experience it. And it leaves a trace, an alive memory is left in me which I can recapture later. This memory is given. To remember myself is memory, yes? But what will remember? It is given to me to remember and I awake again to a sense again of this hidden presence.

So, food. Food of impressions—impressions of myself.

You know, when a journalist comes to interview, say, a potter, and asks him: "Well, could you explain to me how you do that?" If the potter begins to say, "Well, first this and then that . . . and so on," what does it convey? But if the potter goes on with his pot, the answer is there without an explanation—without reducing it to an explanation. It can be perceived. And then the journalist who really is a journalist would also try with his tools to translate what had been perceived into something which could be read. He *saw* the process. But most of the time it is stupidities. I do not know what objective art is, but at least I know that those who pretend to explain are neither artists—nor objective witnesses. Very often we *seem* to understand and very often it's a misappropriation—"Oh yes, *I* understand." It is given me to understand at a moment when I am sensitive to what is offered me. But as soon as I take hold of it, it's finished.

But it's marvelous, isn't it? You know, the person who understands everything always, has an explanation for everything—he's dead!

P. On a larger scale, I'm wondering if you feel there is a relationship between the idea of reciprocal feeding on a cosmic scale and the idea of the three foods.

H.T. Part of it is certainly the question of scale. It cannot be approached without keeping the sense of relativity. In the representation of a human being, for example, it is said that the human mind is thirty thousand times slower than the body. You understand what it means. "Oh, yes, of course." But you don't. It's out of scale for our ordinary way of thinking. We can talk about it—but we do not understand. And there are times we can perceive something corresponding—but there is something which is always late, it comes afterwards. It's a reflection of a reflection—dimmer and dimmer, so slow, and so many things have passed in between. So once again we are in front of this mystery that is far beyond what we are able to conceive of. Yet these questions have a value, provided of course we do not attempt to answer them. But it may be a help to enlarge the scale of our interrogation. What we are given to perceive in our normal surroundings is a reflection of a reflection of a reflection of something much greater and much bigger. It is really of value to understand that what is taking place here is insignificant in a way, and at the same time it is extremely significant for me if I see the other way round. I am a small piece of life which is invisible on this larger scale. So if I begin to *think* about it, and to draw conclusions—I think I need to keep a sense of wonder. When I quote an objective thought from a great thinker, if I just quote it, I spoil it. But if I capture the sense of wonder, I know that I do not understand, but I know that it opens my understanding, it opens it to more—always more. Then I feel myself closer to what was offered.

There are certain formulations I can think of that even if I live twenty more years, I am sure I will not be able to understand. There are things which are unfathomable, but each time it evokes so much in me that it's a rediscovery each time. I don't understand why sometimes we try so hard to get it understood. It would kill something in me. The sense of wonder once again is very much more.

P. There seems to be an appetite of the mind, a kind of greed it has when it is working alone and isolated which wants its own satisfaction without any regard to the rest of the being.

H.T. There is certainly a greed for impressions, but this greed is against a real reception. It is true that the mind has this avidity. Now there is always the possibility of referring to something which is behind. I think that attitudes, outerly expressed by tension—(leans forward, slamming table)— "What do you mean?" For me that means it is finished; it makes it impossible for other impressions to come and to awake corresponding spheres of interest in my mind, in my body, and in my feeling. But these awaken insofar as I am able to remember the amplitude of the gift which is offered me again and again. If I succumb to my ordinary pretenses and greed I lose something; but if I try to keep open to what I know is there, whether I am aware of it or not—it is there. Then there is a natural attempt at keeping open—I keep open. I know that something is offered me over and over again and I try not to be away from it.

P. So there is a kind of fasting which is possible for the mind, a not allowing the greed of the mind, the greed of the feeling, the greed of the body to overtake this openness.

H.T. Yes, fasting. Keeping available for what cannot satisfy my ordinary greed. Memory is there also to help me—a certain kind of memory. Memories are against it most of the time. But there is memory in depth that we can try to open ourselves to once again, and once again. We lack corresponding words—in the same breath we speak of memory and memory, real memory and false memory. But it is there.

5

♦

An Interview with Dr. Yeshi Dhonden
by William Segal

"Sleep," VOL. VII:1, January, 1982

Sleep and the
Inner Landscape

*D*r. *Yeshi Dhonden, who for more than twenty years
served as personal physician to the Dalai Lama, has traveled widely in Europe and
the United States lecturing on the Tibetan science of healing. The following
interview was conducted at the Woodstock, New York, home of Dr. Robert
Thurman, Professor of Religion at Amherst College and a founder of the American
Institute of Buddhist Studies. Dr. Thurman served as translator during the interview.
It was conducted by William Segal, former publisher of* American Fabrics, *who
is an artist, an orientalist and longtime student of Buddhism, especially Zen.*

*Dr. Dhonden was born in Lhasa; he took his novice vows as a Buddhist monk
there at the age of eight. At fourteen, he was admitted to the Astro-Medical
Institute at Lhasa; he studied there for five years under the master physician
Khyenrab Norbu. He then served as an intern for four years, and at the age of
twenty-two began traveling throughout Tibet healing the ill. In 1959, he fled from
Tibet to India, where he settled in Dharamsala, in the Himalayan foothills, where
His Holiness the Dalai Lama has established his exiled government. He founded
the Tibetan Medical Institute there in 1962.*

◆

WILLIAM SEGAL Shakespeare wrote that sleep "knits up the ravell'd sleave
of care." How do you see sleep in a physiological sense?

Dr. YESHI DHONDEN Because it is strenuous for consciousness to be constantly distracted among the gross objects of experience, the return to the subtle level experienced in sleep is extremely beneficial to the consciousness and its relationship to the physical body. Tibetans have certain views of the sleep process which are very complicated, relating to such subjects as death, mantra practices, etc. We analyze and understand the physical body in terms of five elements: the four elements of earth, air, fire, and water; the fifth element is sometimes space, sometimes consciousness, depending on different systems. In that context, when one is awake, the four elements are extremely active and consciousness is very much mixed among the four elements, and throughout the five external sense powers.

Consciousness is distracted by the coarse objects of experience. Therefore when one falls asleep, it is very similar to the death process. That is to say, the six-fold aggregate consciousness, which in its rest stage resides in the heart, withdraws from its sensory activity, and returns into the subtle plane. It is similar to the death experience.

W.S. Sometimes in the waking state one has a clear cognition of one's existence. What happens to the sense of self in sleep, behind all this turmoil and activity which you describe?

Dr. D. The sense of self that we tend to have in the waking state of consciousness is a distorted one. It is a false identification with the coarse objects and elements of experience and the sense realms. When we fall asleep the erroneous, delusory sense of self dissolves into what we call the extremely subtle wind-mind, or neural energy mind (although it literally means wind, breeze, it is a subtle energy).

W.S. What is to be learned in sleep? Is there anything which speaks to the unfulfilled needs of the inner psyche which can carry over from the sleep to the waking state?

Dr. D. It can only be explained by the doctrine of esoteric *Mantrayana* (or *Tantrayana*) which is normally given to initiates in full detail as, for example, in the yoga of sleep. In general, I can say that in the Buddhist view the sleep and death states are similar. The dream state and the between state [between death and rebirth] are similar, and the waking state and the birth state, or the rebirth state, are similar. So the entire life cycle is encapsulated in the cycle of sleep, dream, and waking. Therefore, since the death state and the sleep state are the same, that is the time when one automatically enters into what the Tibetans call the Clear Light. The Clear Light is the experiential description of Ultimate Reality. In death one passes through the Clear Light in a certain way, usually failing to recognize that Clear Light, and thus immediately getting involved in the forms of the next life. In the same way, in the sleep state one automatically enters the Clear Light, as experienced by a very subtle wind-mind. But the sleeping person usually cannot recognize where he is because the connection of the coarse mind and the subtle mind is not consciously traced by the individual. This Clear Light experience which everyone has in sleep, even though it may or may not be recognized, is called the Clear Light experience of the Ground Reality, or the Basis.

It is not a question of saying sleep is this or that, or does this or that. In order to understand sleep, one has to understand the whole arrangement of what is called the Ground, the Path, and the Fruit, as well as the transmutation of the three Bodies into the Path. And the three Bodies of Buddhahood are the *Dharmakāya*, Body of Truth; the *Sambhōgakāya*, Body of Beatitude; and the *Nirmānakāya*, Body of Incarnation. The Body of Truth is assimilated with death and sleep; the Body of Beatitude with dreams and with the between state; and the Body of Incarnation is assimilated with birth and with the waking state. When one understands these different arrangements, and how the coarse and subtle minds fluctuate, how one's sense of self moves between the coarse and subtle minds, then one can understand sleep. But you cannot isolate sleep without understanding the framework.

W.S. Why do many people feel reluctant to interrupt the state of deep, restful sleep?

Dr. D. It is not an invariable thing that people will always like the sleep state. Some people will particularly like it; others will be more attracted to the state of being awake. It depends on which of the "three poisons," the three major mental addictions or habits, called desire, hatred, and delusion, are predominant. The person who is lethargic, who is prone to strong delusion-predominance, will particularly like sleep. Those prone to desire and anger will not necessarily be interested in sleep. It depends on their particular tendency. All this has to do with the cycle of the elements. Perhaps the fundamental reason is connected with the stabilizing element which is called the earth element and the flowing element which is the water element. These two are essential to the universe. That is, they are part of its balance. Fire and wind by themselves will just burn up or fly away. So the normal balance of earth and water is essential to normal existence as we know it. In the context of their normal balance, there is a cycle of the increase and decrease of the respective elements, and what we call sleep is that time when earth and water elements are on the increase and heaviness and stability are increased, as opposed to mobility and energy. So it is an equilibrating phenomenon in relation to the cycle of the elements.

Different living beings have different sleeping habits. Some sleep in the daytime and some sleep at night, some for short and others for long hours. This has to do with the different arrangement of elements of the different beings. Particularly in human beings, the elements manifest in regard to what is known as the three humors. These are the wind, the bile, and the phlegm. When the phlegmatic humor, which relates to earth and water, increases, then heaviness and stability increase. And that happens at night.

If, in fact, this balance is not observed, and we do not allow this time for the increase of the earth and water elements and do not sleep for long periods of time, then those elements become out of balance and we feel the effects. We feel very heavy if we do not sleep for a long time because the earth and water are having an undue imbalancing effect upon our system, inasmuch as they have not had their own free time to increase. Therefore, it is essential that one sleep to keep things in equilibrium.

W.S. How does one prepare oneself for a more beneficial, effective sleep?

DR. D. In general terms, since sleep is caused by a preponderance of the heavy earth and water elements, strong food with some oil in the evening, bringing heaviness and stability to the system, grounds the winds in circulating and absorbing the food and ties up the bile in digestion. But it is essential to realize that one particular mode of behavior or preparation will not necessarily help all persons. There are different kinds of sleep and types of insomnia depending on the constitution and the balance of elements in the individual. Obviously too much tea and black coffee are bad in the evening—especially tea without milk.

W.S. Do you place any emphasis on the time of meditation practice—

before sleep or upon awakening?

DR. D. There are various levels of meditation. If one is in a stage of intensive meditation practice, the morning is the best time. When one's energies are fresh and when one concentrates on a particular point, meditation is most effective in the early morning. Of course those who are highly accomplished in meditation, meditate "without day and night." They never really do sleep or in another sense they always are asleep, because of what I mentioned before where the sleep and the *Dharmakāya*, that it to say the Ultimate Reality, are completely inseparable. In our days it is very hard to find such a thing or even to talk about such a thing.

Returning to the question, usually it is in the morning that we obtain the best results from meditation, although it is also true that if we meditate at the time of falling asleep, we can keep the continuity of our meditation going better and sleep more refreshed. We can even have auspicious or educative dreams by having a certain concentration near the time of falling asleep. However, for us ordinary people, if we're trying to meditate before falling asleep we may go to sleep while meditating!

W.S. In relation to what you just said about educative dreams, who or what can remember the dreams and experiences of sleep? When I wake up, I go back to my mind for memory or recall. What level of mind remembers? Who observes all this show? Who remembers the different states?

DR. D. That again is explained in terms of the different types of consciousness, the subtle and the coarse consciousnesses. In other words the person who remembers, that entity which remembers, is the subtle consciousness which is people's real consciousness. And this subtle consciousness is the one that is present as a continuum throughout all of these states, as indeed, according to the Tibetan view, it links the different lifetimes of sentient beings. Therefore, this subtle consciousness carries the impressions of these previous experiences: the thickness or coarseness of sleep, the deepness or lightness of sleep. There are various kinds of mental turbulences that can interrupt this memory. Otherwise we would remember.

The analysis of different types of consciousness in our scientific texts is precise and elaborate. The rememberer is one's subtle consciousness, which is oneself. In other words, one's coarse self identified with the body is not one's real self.

W.S. Some people remember their dreams. Others do not. Why?

Dr. D. This subject is complex and difficult. The really developed man can be perfectly aware of all his dreams. He has full mobility between the subtle and the coarse states. His memory is infallible. He can remember every kind of experience, even former lives. But that's another question. However, the reason that sometimes ordinary people do not remember is that although they have the same subtle consciousness, the same Clear Light connection, they do not pay attention to it. They have no context with which to understand what is taking place.

Dreams occurring right after falling asleep reflect the process of digestion, and would be highly irrelevant as far as spiritual growth goes. But dreams at the early predawn time, for example, where the system is mostly clear of the evening's food and the channels are more receptive to the passage of the subtle energies, can be very illuminating. Sometimes they reveal the future and other things. Training the mobility of the subtle consciousness, and developing a relative mastery of it in its different states, is the way to develop special powers. Again, it is a difficult subject. But it is very precise and sophisticated. It is technically explained in our texts.

W.S. Is there a way of measuring or categorizing dreams? Or is there a way in which we can have an influence on the powers of dreaming?

Dr. D. It is not a question of measurement since these are qualitative types of experiences. However, since there are eight channels in the central heart complex, the way in which the winds dissolve and surge through the different interconnecting passages has do to with posture in sleeping. If you sleep crouched up in certain ways, certain sides will be closed off. The ideal position for sleep, in the sense that it keeps the eight channels balanced and does not cramp one exclusively, is to lie on the right side in what is known as the "lion posture." It is better not to put pressure on the heart. There is a definite connection between posture and the type of inner landscape travel happening in sleep.

W.S. If there is a different time-space continuum in sleep and if transformation of energy continually goes on in our lives, how are these transformations related to our time and space?

Dr. D. First, subtle energy-wind-mind never dies, ever. It continues always. What is really meant is that all beings have a Buddha nature or that a Buddha essence is in every being. It never disappears. If one body dies, the Buddha essence simply takes up residence in another body. Continuity is maintained through death. However, for ordinary beings, this realization slips by without being noticed either in sleep or in death. It takes up another "between state" and another rebirth. One just passes right by the realization, hardly noticing the time of complete subtleness when one is really totally in contact with it. Therefore, a definition of a subtle level of Buddhahood—not only having a Buddha essence, but the actual conscious flowering of Buddhahood—is the realization that the subtle mind is completely indivisible from the Clear Light Reality, a conscious experience which you could call timeless, infinite, or spaceless. Certainly it is beyond the ordinary sense of relativity and of time and space.

In the coarse forms and time-subjected realities, we have different senses of space and time. According to how stressful our existence is, time will seem slower. If our time is unstressful, relaxed as in a godly realm, time will go quickly. Space similarly. If we have a certain type of vision, large space will seem small to us; if we have another type, small spaces will seem huge. Then there is another interesting point: how do our ordinary human bodies on this earthly plane relate the subtle conscious energy to our reality? In the back of the heart *chakra*, heart complex, there is a space inside the central channel, a kind of chamber that is sealed off in the ordinary person by certain knots in the channels. It is only a Buddha who has it opened. The subtle consciousness energy can go in and out of that chamber and there is no difference between that chamber and the rest of his being. For us, it is a closed-off chamber where there exists something similar to a treasure box. In this resides a drop, another little treasure box, inside of which the jewel is the extremely subtle consciousness.

When an ordinary person dies, these knots unravel and that jewel will travel until it finds another storehouse, another place of residing. For example, in rebirth it enters the drops of the father and mother in the womb of the mother. This little drop carrying this gem of indestructible subtle consciousness will enter the two drops of the father and mother (in the womb) from the between state. Birth is expressed in the form of the union of the three drops—the white drop of the father, the red drop of the mother, and the blue drop of energy consciousness. The three will combine and that will be rebirth. Around the combination of those three drops the whole body and whole being will evolve. That central point where the rebirth took place will be at the very center of the heart. It is an esoteric explanation of birth.

w.s. How to open this inner chamber during one's lifetime? Is it a question of discipline and practice? Can we approach it from a physiological point of view?

Dr. D. This consciousness sits in its seat like a jewel within a kind of mandala place, or mansion. It has in itself no obstruction. It can travel anywhere. There is no need to open any doorway—it is completely open. It is there. It is perfect in itself. It is home in a way. There is no question of opening it up.

w.s. At the same time, mankind is afflicted with suffering and pain. If it is as you say, why isn't the path more readily apparent, more readily available?

Dr. D. This consciousness in the ordinary person is unrecognized. Everyone has it, but no one recognizes that he has it. People identify themselves with their coarse-level consciousness. Even though this subtle level of consciousness is enshrined there, people do not notice it. They can even go through death, where in fact the coarse level of consciousness is dissolved, and they still don't recognize it. They are drawn into creating a new coarse-level involvement in the between state and then in the future birth state. That's why in our science of dying—in *The Tibetan Book of the Dead*—the essential issue is to bring the dying person face to face with the Clear Light Reality—to appropriate their own subtle reality as their reality—rather than simply jump off into another coarse reality. Now the way of doing that is not effective for someone who identifies with the gross reality and with his possessions. Therefore there is something known as the Path-level Reality. The Path-level Clear Light is the Clear Light where they begin to build up the bridges between the Ground-level coarse reality and the death state Ultimate Reality. They begin to get used to it and merge into it. One can talk about this in an esoteric way and as a physiological process. However, it is more usual to talk about it in terms of a mental process, which is in fact the mind-realization of the nature of Ultimate Reality. We call it direct intuitive wisdom which directly understands emptiness and directly experiences emptiness, which is the ultimate nature of reality.

In this direct experience of emptiness, the critical wisdom penetrates, drilling through the apparent solidity of the coarse-level reality, seeing its insubstantiality, and ceasing to find anything with which to identify. In the process of coming to that true intuitive wisdom, one joins with one's own subtle level consciousness until finally one uses it to know directly the emptiness which is the nature of Ultimate Reality. When the subtle consciousness, directly from the heart, experiences this emptiness of intrinsic substantiality, then one has achieved one's own Buddhahood. At that time this subtle consciousness can know everything. One has abilities such as reading other people's minds. That is why it is said that there is no obstruction at all to Buddha's omniscience. Buddha's mind is omniscient because it is the subtle consciousness that can be anywhere without obstruction. And that never dies, that never dies.

W.S. Would awareness of emptiness, in the waking state, carry on in the dream state?

DR. D. Yes, for someone who has a profound realization of emptiness. If one were to have that, then one would be in a state where the Clear Light would be manifested either waking or dreaming or sleeping with no separation among the three.

However, it is necessary to make clear that emptiness is not a dualistic state, a sort of nothingness that is the opposite of the manifest appearance. You are not cut off from experiencing. This is important since Westerners tend to feel that emptiness means a sort of nothingness.

W.S. Perhaps all this depends on a sort of continuous awareness and capacity to hold one's attention on what one could say is one's subtle nature. In other words, if one is distracted by body, mind, feelings, one fails to remember this subtle consciousness. Could you verify this?

DR. D. In general what you say is correct. Basically, the essence of Buddhism is not trying to find something one doesn't have, but simply to recover what one does have but doesn't know. However, one should be clear. What is involved is a difficult process because of the intensity and the type of the distractions. When you say distractions, you are saying a great deal.

There is a very powerful, fully elaborated path which pacifies distraction. For example, the only way to radically pacify distraction on the gross level is not simply to suppress awareness of the gross-level reality. By fully confronting the gross-level reality and looking at it with critical, penetrating wisdom, one sees its true nature. This is not at all a *quieting* of the mind, but an *intensifying* of the mind's analytic, penetrating functioning— like a scientific analysis. It is actually an intensifying of the investigating process. There is much more involved in an awareness of the deepest nature than a simple suppression of obvious mental manifestations which we would think of as distractions.

w.s. Is it true that all human beings are close to Buddhahood?

Dr. D. I certainly think that from the Buddhist point of view the human being is incredibly close to evolutionary perfection, which is called Buddhahood. It is so in the sense that in a single life, if a human being practices assiduously and has the teachings, he can actually transform himself from an ordinary human being into a perfectly enlightened being.

There are many forms of life within the ocean of evolution that are much less suited than human beings to the pursuit of this perfection of enlightenment. That is why Tibetan Buddhism stresses that people use this precious human life to the very fullest to achieve evolutionary perfection, or Buddhahood. To waste this pinnacle of human life and to fall back to the lower orders rather than to obtain Buddhahood is a tremendous waste. We accept the nearness of the human being to Buddhahood. Any system which says that humans cannot understand, that only God or other super-beings can understand, is repressive of the full potential of the human being and does not agree with the Tibetan Buddhist view.

w.s. What do you think of the recent Western experiments and investigations into sleep and dreams? What would be a right path to pursue?

Dr. D. EEG charting waves, measurements of dreams, all this can only give superficial information. One only learns about the currents which move in the body. It is a vague and unreliable approach which is not particularly exciting. There is no need at all to wear out machinery and brains. We have an existing record of thousands of years of experiment, already there, that needs to be studied. To spend money on big machines merely to start experiments and not to fully study Tibetan texts—this is unfortunate. There are thousands of pages cataloguing the different states of sleep and types of dreams; this study would be fruitful for scientists and researchers. There are plenty of these texts in American university libraries. You only need people who can read them. Everything is here.

6

♦

An Interview with Peter Brook

"Mask and Metaphor," VOL. VII:3, August, 1981

Lie and Glorious Adjective

*P*eter Brook *is internationally known for his work in theater, opera, and cinema. He was born in London in 1925, took his M.A. at Oxford, and later received an honorary doctorate in literature from Birmingham University. Other honors include the title of Commander of the Order of the British Empire and Officier des Arts et Lettres. His films, several of which have won international honors, include* Lord of the Flies *(1963),* Marat/Sade *(1967),* King Lear *(1969), and* Meetings with Remarkable Men *(1979). The New York stage saw his production of* A Midsummer Night's Dream *in 1971, a bill of four plays at La Mama (which included the magical* Conference of the Birds*) in 1980, and in 1983* La Tragédie de Carmen*. His most recent triumph is a nine-hour version of the epic of* The Mahabharata.

It is an impressive history, and only a partial sketch of an enormously productive career. But Brook is more than energetic. He is an original. Anyone seriously interested in theater is interested in what Brook is doing, for his work is at the living, leading edge of the art. But it is not the extraordinary quality and variety, or even the brilliance, of Brook's work that makes the greatest claim on our attention; rather, it is its innovative courage, the relentlessness of its drive to come closer and closer to the heart of truth. This same quality is evidenced in the total attention he gives to listening as well as to speaking. Behind his fluency and humor, one feels the intensity, as well as the speed, with which a thought is at once followed and disciplined, like a trained hunting dog, turned loose on the scent but never out of reach of its owner's eye and voice.

PARABOLA I was talking with Arthur Amiotte about the idea of masks, and he suggested that it went beyond the mask itself and included the whole idea of something "in the image of. . . . " What can you tell us about masks in the theater?

PETER BROOK It's obvious that there are masks and masks. There is something very noble, very mysterious, very extraordinary, which is the mask, and something disgusting, something really sordid, nauseating (and very common to the Western art theater) which is also called a mask. They are similar because they are both things you put on your face, but they are as different as health and disease. There is a mask which is life-giving, that affects the wearer and the observer in a very positive way; and there is another thing that can be put on on the face of a distorted human being that makes him even more distorted. And both go under the same name, "masks," and to the casual observer look very similar. I think it has now become an almost universally accepted cliché that we all wear masks all the time; but the moment one accepts that as being true, and begins to ask oneself questions about it, one sees that the usual facial expression either conceals (so it's a mask in that sense) that it's not in tune with what is really going on inside, or it is a decorated account: it presents the inner process in a more flattering or attractive light; it gives a lying version. A weak person puts on a strong face, or vice versa. The everyday expression is a mask in the sense that it's either a concealment or a lie; it is not in harmony with the inner movement. So if one's face is operating so well as a mask, what's the purpose of putting on another face?

But in fact, if one takes these two categories, the horrible mask and the good mask, one sees that they operate in quite different ways. The horrible mask is the one most continually used in the Western theater. What happens here is that an individual, usually a scene designer, is asked to design a mask. He works from one thing only, which is his own subjective fantasy; what else can he do? So someone sits in front of a drawing board and draws out of his own subconscious one of his own million lying or distorted or sentimental masks and then pops it onto another person. So you have something that in a way is even worse than one's own lie—one is lying through the external image of someone else's lie. However, what is worse yet is that because another person's lie comes not from the surface but from the subconscious, it is basically even nastier, because you are lying through another person's fantasy life. And that is where almost all masks that you see, in the ballet and so on, have something morbid about them; because it is an aspect of the subjective subconscious—frozen. So you have this picture impression of something inanimate and basically belonging to the hidden area of personal hang-ups and frustrations.

Now the traditional mask works exactly the other way round. The traditional mask in essence isn't a "mask" at all, because it is an image of the essential nature. In other words, a traditional mask is a portrait of a man without a mask.

For instance, the Balinese masks that we used in *The Conference of the Birds* are realistic masks, in the sense that, unlike the African masks, the features are not distorted; they are completely naturalistic. What one sees is that the person who designs them, exactly like the person who sculpts the heads in Bunraku, has behind him thousands of years of tradition in which human types are observed with *such* precision that you can see that if the craftsman reproducing them, generation after generation, goes one millimeter to the right or to the left, he is no longer reproducing the essential type but a personal value. But if he is absolutely true to this traditional knowledge—which you could call a traditional psychological classification of man, an absolute knowledge of the essential types—you find that what is called a mask should be called an anti-mask. The traditional mask is an actual portrait, a soul-portrait, a photograph of what you rarely see, only in truly evolved human beings: an outer casing that is a complete and sensitive reflection of the inner life. So because of this, in a mask carved in such a way, whether a Bunraku head or a Balinese realistic mask, the first characteristic is that there is nothing morbid about it. There is no impression, even when you see one hanging on the wall, of a shrunken head—no impression of death. It is not a death mask. On the contrary, these masks, although motionless, seem to be breathing life. Provided the actor goes through certain steps that we will talk about in a moment, the moment he wears the mask it becomes alive in an infinite number of ways. A mask of this order has this extraordinary characteristic that the moment it is on a human head, if the human being inside is sensitive to its meaning, it has an absolutely inexhaustible quantity of expressions. We found this while we were rehearsing with them. When the mask is hanging on the wall, a person could—crudely and falsely—put adjectives to it, saying, "Ah, this is the proud man." You put the mask on, and you can no longer say, "This is the proud man," because it could have looks of humility, it could have humility sliding into gentleness; those vast staring eyes can express aggressivity or they can express fear; it is endlessly, endlessly shifting—but *within* the purity and intensity of the unmasked man whose deepest inner nature is constantly revealing itself, while the masked man's inner nature is continuously concealed. So in that way, I think the first basic paradox is that the true mask is the expression of somebody unmasked.

P. What effect does it have on the person wearing it?

P.B. I will speak from my experience with the Balinese masks, but I have to go back one step before that. One of the first, knockout exercises you can do with actors, which is used in lots of theater schools where they use masks, is putting a plain, blank, white mask on someone. The moment you take someone's face away in that way, it's the most electrifying impression: suddenly to find oneself knowing that that thing one lives with, and which one knows is transmitting something all the time, is no longer there. It's the most extraordinary sense of liberation. And the awakening of a body awareness is immediately there with it, irresistibly; so that if you want to make an actor aware of his body, instead of explaining it to him and saying, "You have a body and you need to be aware of it," just put a bit of white paper on his face and say, "Now look around." He can't fail to be instantly aware of everything he normally forgets, because all the attention has been released from this great magnet up top.

Now to go back to the Balinese masks. When they arrived, the Balinese actor who was with us laid them out. All the actors, like children, threw themselves on the masks, put them on, started roaring with laughter, looking at one another, looking in the mirror, fooling around—having a ball, like children when you open up the dressing-up hamper. I looked at the Balinese actor. He was appalled; he was standing there shell-shocked— because for him the masks were sacred. He gave me a pleading look, and I stopped everybody short and just said a couple of words to remind everyone that these weren't just things out of a Christmas cracker. And because our group had worked long enough under different forms, the potential respect was there; it was just that in our typical Western way, one forgets; everybody was too over-enthusiastic and excited, but at the tiniest reminder they came back right away. But it was quite clear that within a matter of minutes the masks were being completely desacralized—because the masks will play any game you want, and what was interesting was that before I stopped them, when everyone was fooling around with them, the masks themselves appeared to be not much better than what you get out of a Christmas cracker—because that was what was being invested in them. A mask is two-way traffic all the time; it sends a message in and projects a message out. It operates by the laws of echoes: if the chamber is perfect, the sound going in and the one going out are reflections; there is a perfect relation between the echo chamber and the sound; but if it isn't, it is like a distorted mirror. Here, when the actors sent back a distorted response, the mask itself took on a distorted face. The minute they started again, with quiet and respect, the masks looked different and the people inside them *felt* different.

The great magic of the mask, which every actor receives from it, is that he *can't* tell what it looks like on him; he can't tell what impression he is making—and yet he knows. You somehow do and don't know, on a rational level; but the sensitivity to the mask exists in another way, and it's something that develops.

One of the techniques they use in Bali which is very interesting is that the Balinese actor starts by looking at a mask, holding it in his hands. He looks at it for a long while, until he and the mask begin to become like a reflection of each other; he begins to feel it partly as his own face—but not totally, because in another way he goes towards *its* independent life. And gradually he begins to move his hand so that the mask takes on a life, and he is watching it—he sort of empathizes with it. And then something may happen which none of our actors could even attempt (and it rarely happens even with the Balinese actor) which is that the breathing begins to modify; he begins to breathe differently with each mask. It's obvious, in a way, that each mask represents a certain type of person, with a certain body and a certain tempo and inner rhythms, and so a certain breathing; as he begins to feel this and as his hand begins to take a corresponding tension, the breath changes till a certain *weight* of breathing begins to penetrate the actor's whole body; and when that is ready, he puts on the mask. And the whole shape is there.

Our actors can't do it that way—and shouldn't, because that belongs to a whole tradition and training. But in a different way, because they can't play on that sort of highly developed instrument of technique, they can develop something through pure sensitivity, with no knowledge of what are right or wrong forms. The actor takes the mask, studies it, and as he puts it on, his face slightly modifies itself until it goes towards the shape of .the mask, and in a way he has dropped one of his own masks; so the intervening flesh-masks disappear and the actor is in close contact, epidermal contact, with a face that is not his face, but the face of a very strong, essential type of man. And his actor's capacity to be a comedian (without which he couldn't be an actor) makes him realize his potentiality to *be* that person. That becomes *his* role; and the moment it is assumed, it comes to life, it is no longer hard and fast but something that adapts itself to any circumstance.

P. So is it possible for a Western actor to act in these Balinese masks? What happens?

P.B. It is exactly the same as playing a role—exactly the same. A role is a meeting, a meeting between an actor as a mass of potentialities—and a catalyst. Because a role is a form of catalyst, from outside; it makes a demand, and draws into form the unformed potentiality of the actor. That is why the meeting between an actor and a role always produces a different result. Take a great role, like Hamlet: the nature of Hamlet on one hand makes an absolutely specific set of demands; the words are there and don't change from generation to generation. But at the same time, like a mask, although it looks as though it is set in its form, it is exactly the reverse. In fact, it's something which, because it operates like a catalyst, when it encounters the human material which is the individual actor, it creates all the time new specifics. This meeting between the demand coming from the outside, which is the role that the actor is assuming, and the individuality of the actor, produces always a new series of combinations. So an oriental actor, a Balinese for example, if he has the basic sensitivity, understanding, openness, wish, etc., can play Hamlet; and a great Balinese actor, bringing the whole of his human understanding to the part of Hamlet, *must* produce, second by second, something totally different from John Gielgud approaching the same thing, because it is a different meeting in different circumstances. But in each case, a truth of equal quality and of equal value can appear. In exactly the same way, a great mask put on a Balinese or on an American or on a Frenchman, given the same basic conditions of skill, sensitivity, and sincerity, should produce results qualitatively equal, but in terms of form, totally different.

P. That makes me wonder: is there a difference in the use of mask in ritual and the use of masks in theater, where you are performing for different reasons?

P.B. I think it goes through stages. I go back to the concrete experience we had: *The Conference of the Birds*, and why we *had* to use masks. We have always avoided them; I loathe masks in the theater, and I have never used them before, because every time I have even touched them it has been either Western masks or the idea of getting somebody to make masks, and I have always shied away from the idea of putting subjectivity onto subjectivity, which makes no sense at all. So in place of masks we have done everything with the actor's face—what better instrument do you have? But what we did up to the first time that we used masks was to work so that the actor's individuality appeared through his face; and that work is, by one technique or another, getting rid of his superficial masks. It would be virtually impossible to take a successful television character, let's say, and get his individuality to appear without a grueling and perhaps highly dangerous process of smashing his masks, because his identification with certain successful facial expressions is so deeply ingrained, and so much part of his way of life and his stake in the world, that he couldn't let it go. But a young actor, for instance, who wants to develop, can recognize and eliminate his stereotypes—to a degree; and in doing so his face becomes a better mirror—in the way a Sufi would talk about his mirror becoming more polished, a cleaner mirror of what is happening inside his face. You see in many people that their faces reflect more rather than less of what is inside them. The use of the actor undisguised, without makeup, without costume, has been the trend of the experimental theater for the last twenty years or so; it has been to let the actor's nature appear— and one also sees that in the very best film acting; the actor uses on the surface what he has deep inside him, and he allows the flicker of an eyelid to be a sensitive mirror of what is happening inside him. In that way, through training that doesn't go towards using an actor's *personality*, but on the contrary towards letting his personality make way for his *individuality*, the use of the face in a sensitive way makes the face less of a mask and more a reflector of that individuality.

However, we found—which is why we turned to masks—that there is a point where the actor's individuality comes up against his own natural human limitations. A talented actor can improvise up to the level of his talent. But that doesn't mean that he can improvise King Lear, because his talent doesn't reach beyond his normal range of experience to *that* range. So he can't improvise King Lear, but he can *meet* King Lear if the role is given to him. In the same way, an actor can improvise with his face, and that will reflect anything within his normal circle of emotions, responses, and experiences. But for instance, if in *The Conference of the Birds* I ask one of our actors to find the face that corresponds with an old dervish, the leap is too great. He can have the beginning of an intellectual understanding of what it is about, he can have a beginning of respect for what that could mean, but he hasn't got what is needed to be able, unaided, to turn his face into the illuminated face of an old dervish. He can go, let's say, one step in a direction that needs a thousand steps. And it is at that point that you see that the skill of one of our actors (obviously one has to face the reality unpretentiously) can't equal the skill of the carver of the mask fed by a thousand years of tradition. So for our actor to be able to say, "There was once an old dervish. . . . " by putting on the traditional mask he leaps a light year ahead, because he is drawn immediately by the mask to something he can understand when it is given to him, but he can't creatively impose on himself.

To connect with your idea of ritual: In terms of theater, in *The Conference of the Birds* we used birds when we saw that a big, fat actor flapping his hands doesn't convey flight as well as it can be conveyed, momentarily, by his holding a little object and suggesting flight with it, when for a moment what you want is the image of flight; but at another moment you don't want that, you want the humanity of the person and then you come back to the actor. In the same way we found, having rehearsed with and without masks (which is why we put them on and off), that there were moments when the natural ordinary reality of the actor is better than the masks; because you don't want all the time the exalted impression. It is like using adjectives: there are moments when a good style is naked and uses very simple words, and there is a moment when without a glorious adjective the sentence can't make its point; and the mask is suddenly a glorious adjective that exalts the entire sentence.

Now, we are talking here all the time about masks that in their very nature are so-called realistic, naturalistic masks. And what amazed me when I saw the Balinese masks for the first time was to see that although they come from a very specific, local culture, they don't actually look primarily oriental. When you look at those masks you see, first and foremost, Old Man—Beautiful Girl—Sad Man—Astonished Man—and then only secondarily, you see: oh yes, they are oriental. This is why we could actually do something which in theory is impossible, which is to use a Balinese mask to express a Persian story—which from a purist point of view would be called shocking, scandalous, a total disregard of tradition. In theory, yes; but once one is dealing with certain essential strands, it is like in cooking—things that in theory you can't combine, in practice can be combined very well. In this case, because these masks were expressing certain specific *but universal* human characteristics, the two go together like bread and butter.

On the other hand, when you are dealing with non-naturalistic masks, you are dealing with something very delicate. Non-naturalistic masks, I think, again fall into two categories. There are the masks that are so strictly coded that they are like a series of words in a foreign language—so highly ritualized that unless you know the language of the signs, you lose nine-tenths of its meaning. Some African or New Guinea masks, for instance, have something very impressive about them, but one can very easily miss the real force of what those masks are saying unless one knows the whole tradition that is behind them and the context in which they are appearing. And I think it is very easy for us to sentimentalize our approach to masks, the way people do who buy one just to hang it on the wall. It is a beautiful wall decoration, but what a degraded use of something whose signs, if read, are something infinitely more significant!

But there is another type of mask, where these two categories overlap: one that in a specific way is also reflecting inner experience, but not inner *psychological* experience. In other words, you can say that there is the type of mask that we have been talking about so far, which shows fundamental psychological types of man through very exact, realistic description of his features. And that is a concealed man that is being shown. But then you can say that there is another concealed inner man, that could be called the essential deity inside each person. So you have, for instance, a mask that is the expression of maternity—the mask that expresses the fundamental maternal principle. Now, that expression goes beyond the picture of the benign mother, which one sees in paintings of the Virgin and child. You go from that to the icon, for instance, where there is something more fundamental; the essential quality is there in something that is no longer reflected naturalistically, where the proportions begin to change, until you get into all the range of statues with eyes five times bigger than the nose and so on—and within that, there is a form of mask that is ritualized and is on a knife-edge of having a possible theatrical use. This is just the area where these two categories overlap. There is the mask which doesn't look like a face in the normal sense of the word—like in a Picasso painting with five sets of eyes on top of the other and three flat noses—yet which, worn by a person sensitive to its nature, still expresses an aspect of the human condition, in a way beyond the capacity of any actor to show, because no actor can exalt himself to that degree. It is just like the difference between straight speech, and some declamation, and chant: these are all steps toward a more powerful, essential, less everyday expression which still can be totally real if it reflects a truth of human nature. And in that way it is possible to use masks—but that is something *so* delicate. We have one Balinese mask of that sort, a very ferocious sort of demon mask, and we have just used it amongst ourselves in rehearsal, with everybody feeling the incredible forces that are let loose just by putting it on—and that there one is going into a big area. For instance, in the *Mahabharata*, we had to find the theatrical version of presenting a god. It is quite clear that an ordinary actor pretending to be a god is ridiculous. One sees that even in productions of *The Tempest* where a lot of girls try to be goddesses; *The Tempest* is usually a disaster. So you have to turn to something that can help you, and the first thing is a mask that contains forces in it and evokes stronger forces than the actor can evoke himself. I have never seen them used in the Western theater in this way, and I think it is something very dangerous for us to approach without a lot of experiment and understanding. In the East or in Africa, this kind of mask is used more in ritual but in a sense for the same purpose, which is to bring into the open abstract things that otherwise are just called forces, so that they take on flesh and blood.

Now that I've talked for an hour, I think I can put into one phrase more simply what I've been trying to say all along: the naturalistic mask expresses essential human types, and the non-naturalistic mask embodies forces.

P. How do you see the danger you were speaking of? Can you specify exactly?

P.B. It's a funny sort of danger. Masks really do radiate power; and if someone is sufficiently sensitive to them, he's not likely to use them badly; but it's possible, and there could be psychic dangers from using something too strong for you. On the other hand, with somebody insensitive to them, it's like a thief stealing from an altar: the chances are not that he'll be punished by a thunderbolt, but just that whoever desecrates something simply contributes his little drop to pulling the world a little lower. So I think the greatest danger is just cheapening.

P. The man is also in that danger.

P.B. Yes, of being cheapened.

P. Returning to my former question: it seems the mask can really have an effect on the wearer, and at least for the moment it is worn it is a sort of transforming agent.

P.B. Absolutely.

P. Can it have more than a momentary effect, do you think?

P.B. It depends on what people bring to it.

P. Do you remember Max Beerbohm's *The Happy Hypocrite*? It was about a man who is horribly, painfully, ugly, so ugly that he shocks and frightens people. So he wears a mask with the face of a beautiful saint; and he tries very hard to conform himself to this mask, and to *be* the beautiful saint. Then—I can't remember whether it is the woman he falls in love with, or who it is, but someone realizes that he is wearing a mask and tears it off his face. He is crushed at the thought that his real ugliness is now revealed—and then, to his amazement, the other person says, "But why did you wear a mask when it is just like your own face?" He has become what the mask represented.

P.B. That's marvelous. But you know, what is interesting is that, like a lot of great basic stories, it could exist in two versions. It could have the other ending, and be a negative story; and I'm sure if you look through the different traditions you would find both: the one that when the mask is pulled off, he is left as a sort of angry monster, because in all those years he only wanted the appearance of saintliness—he never really wanted sufficiently to go all the way; so when the mask goes, he is a Caliban again. And the other ending, the beautiful one, which is that he has lived it so truly that when it is taken away, he is still what he seemed before. The story could be expressed with two different possibilities that are always there, in the degree to which the wearer is responsible to his mask.

P. I was just thinking along those lines: suppose that there *is* an ideal mask—a mask of the ideal mother or father or any other human relation—the objective *fact* of a relationship. What could take the place of a mask, in real life, if one wished to conform oneself to this objective fact, this sort of paradigm of a relation? Is there such a thing in real life? What would a real-life mask be?

P.B. I think that there is something extremely interesting here—which is that the mask is an *apparent* immobilizing of elements that in nature are in movement. It is very curious; the whole question of the life or death of the mask is there. A mask is like a frame of a movie of a running horse: it puts into *apparently* static form something which in fact, viewed in the proper way, is the expression of something in movement. So motherly love is shown as a static expression; but the real-life equivalent is an action, not an expression. To go back to the icon: if we wanted to show a real-life woman with the equivalent of what the icon is reflecting, we would not try to find a woman whose face or whose look toward a child has that expression, but we might follow Mother Teresa, from behind, with a camera, as she goes through her hospital. And it would be through the actions over a stretch of time that one would find the equivalent. It would be certain attitudes, movements, relationships in *time*; so that motherly love in life is not a snapshot, but an action or a series of actions in time, within a duration. And there seems to be a denial of time in the compression of that into an *apparently* frozen form, in a mask, or a painting, or a statue; but the glory of it, when it is on a certain level of quality, is that the frozenness is only a delusion, which disappears the moment the mask is put again on a human face, because then one sees this curious characteristic of its having endless movement contained within it.

P. It's extraordinary how a Bunraku puppet also changes its expression when it is moved.

P.B. But look at the greatest example of all—and heaven help any actor who tries to use it in the theater—the great Buddha statues, those vast stone Buddhas in the Himalayas, for instance. There is a head which is a human head, because it has eyes, and nose, and mouth, and cheeks; it sits on a neck; it has all the characteristics of a mask; it is not made out of flesh and blood but other material, it isn't alive, and it's motionless. On the other hand, is it concealing inner nature? Not a bit of it; it is the highest impression one knows of the expression of inner nature. Is it naturalistic? Not quite, because we don't know anybody who looks quite like the Buddha; but is it fantasized? No; you couldn't even say it is idealized— and yet it is not like any human being one knows. It is a potential—a human being totally fulfilled and realized. The mask is there in repose, but is not like a dead person; on the contrary, it is the repose of something in which the currents of life are circulating all the time, over thousands of years. And it's quite clear that if you took one of those Buddhas and sliced off the head and hollowed it out and made it into a mask, and put it on an actor, either the actor would pull it down—because of his incapacity to support that head—or he would rise up to it. Therefore it would be an absolutely exact measure of the level of his potential understanding. Each person, even with the help of the mask, can go only so far, and a young acolyte wearing the mask would express something quite different from the great master. So the mask would be pulled down or the person would be pulled up exactly, scientifically, in accordance with what he has and what he brings.

This is very much the way possession takes place among the Yorubas. In their tradition, when you assume the role that you are inhabited, you have to rise to meet what is inhabiting you, and you serve the god to the degree that you can consciously bring to him. So again, a beginner inhabited by a god will dance differently, and express something different, from the master. It is exactly the same relation with the mask.

P. Then the question we asked before, about the difference between theater and ritual, depends on the person practicing them?

P.B. Yes, that's it. There are some fascinating masks from Korea and

Bhutan, both of which are quite different from the Balinese. Some of them are completely antinaturalistic, and yet at the same time they are actors' masks that aren't just making coded statements. For instance, the makeup in the Kathakali is more a coded statement that a human expression—you know, a red nose and great streaks across the face—like in the Japanese masks also. Those masks are what I would call cultural masks; they are not the expression of a human impulse, but of cultural fact.

It's very interesting to see that behind a cultural expression there is either this very specific, intellectual code, or something that is still specific but universal, so it can be touched by any human being anywhere and make the same impression, like certain very simple melodies that can really be felt and understood. We found that you have to come to melodies and rhythms of one or two notes to be at the point which is most universally understandable. At the other end of the scale, you have something like contemporary Western music, which is in its way as intellectual as these body paintings, and you have to know the whole intellectual structure to understand it. Without that you really can't feel it directly.

P. It's interesting that the mask is used both for concealment and for revelation. It does seem to do both.

P.B. It liberates the person by taking away their habitual forms, as we were saying before; and that's related to an experience I had in Rio. When I was in Brazil I asked a lot of questions about what possession was among the Macumba and others. Their possession, unlike the Yorubas but just like in Haiti, seems entirely based on the person losing all consciousness. I asked a very sophisticated young priest in Bahia whether it was possible for them to retain any consciousness at all when they are possessed, and he said, "No, thank God!"

In Rio I went one night to a ceremony—it was a Friday night, when there were about nine thousand little ceremonies on all the little back streets. This was on a *very* little back street—I was taken by a local girl who knew her way—and here one went into the equivalent of a sort of nonconformist church, in voodoo terms. It was a little room with rows of chairs laid out rather like a mission hall, and people waiting, and numbers were called out. When you come in, you ask to have your name put down, you are given a number, and when that number is called by somebody with a little loudspeaker, you go to the end of the room where there is something like the altar part of a little chapel, but where in fact nine people are standing. They are all local people who do this once a week in a state of possession: each one is possessed regularly by the same god. So you go up to the particular god you want to have a word with—like a confessional without a box—and just speak for as long as you want. The interesting thing is that there are these local people, who have become sort of specialized in it, who are in a state of pure possession; and its very extraordinary, because they clearly have absolutely no clue as to what's going on; it's totally effaced from their memory. They are all smoking cigars (which is a great characteristic of these particular gods—they all like cigars) so men and women are all puffing away, and talking both normally and yet with certain bizarre characteristics that belong to the god— breaking out with strange sounds. So you ask advice, and the person will tell you what to do. I went and talked to a lady who was possessed, not by a god but by a saint—a man of the parish who died twenty or thirty years ago and became a saint, and returns and inhabits this lady. We had a nice little chat; she was very interested in the coat I was wearing and said, "Es impermeable?" So we were having this chat, and she blessed me and blew smoke all over me, and because it was in Portuguese I couldn't get very far, but something suddenly struck me as I looked around at the other people who were having long conversations. I suddenly realized that the fact that one knew that the person was possessed—and so whatever else was in the eyes looking at you, in a sense quite normally, they couldn't contain subjective judgment—gave you such a freedom! Obviously the Catholic church provides the same freedom by hiding the face of the person you are confessing to. But here you could look the person straight in the eyes, because you knew that although you would see this little lady, who was maybe your neighbor, in the street the next day, *she*—her subjectivity—was *not* looking at you through those eyes; she had become in that sense a mask, and it freed you to say absolutely anything. I felt if I had been able to speak Portuguese, I could have told her anything at all, just like that.

The moment the mask absolves you in that way, the fact that it gives you something to hide behind makes it unnecessary for you to hide. That is the fundamental paradox that exists in all acting: that because you are in safety, you can go into danger. It is very strange, but all theater is based on that. Because there is a greater security, you can take greater risks; and because here it is *not* you, and therefore everything about you is hidden, you can let yourself appear. And that is what the mask is doing: the thing you are most afraid of losing, you lose right away—your ordinary defenses, your ordinary expressions, your ordinary face that you hide behind; and now you hide a hundred percent, because you know that the person looking at you doesn't think it is *you*, and on account of that you can come right out of your shell. We are so imprisoned, also, in such a narrow repertory that even if part of us wanted to, we actually *can't* open our eyes or furrow our brows or move our mouths and cheeks beyond certain limits. And suddenly we are given the capacity to do it: we open our eyes wider and raise our eyebrows higher than we ever have before.

P. We have talked about masks as being liberating, but how about the kind we do wear all the time unawares, which are certainly enslaving?

P.B. Oh, yes! And I think that the use of artists' masks is enslaving for the same reason. But there is the other sort of mask, where you go deliberately *not* towards a liberation; on the contrary, you take some characteristic that you are not very proud of and have it brought out in its most monstrous form. In that sense, there have been contemporary masks that are quite interesting. Joe Chaikin did a play called *Motel*, about two people making love in a motel, who wore masks like caricature heads out of *The New Yorker*, with unchangeable, fixed expressions. No matter what they were doing, the expression remained the same. The woman was a terrible blonde, with a great idiotic face, and the man a sort of salesman type with a goamy expression. These are perhaps the most successful of the contemporary masks; they come out of something contemporary art is qualified to talk about!

P. What about the necessity of masks? The traditional mask is the face of a real man; but we don't have that, so we have to wear some kind of false face—we can't do otherwise. Is there such a thing as being unmasked?

P.B. I don't think that with human beings you take masks off; I think they dissolve through growth, which is a very different thing. There is a lot of talk about stripping off masks, but in fact it is either a very dangerous process or one that doesn't work at all. I think they can thin out and disappear with a process of growth. And I would say that the more evolved a person is, the less easy it is to imitate that person in the caricature sense of the word. If you compare someone whose *personality* is evolved, like Churchill, it is God's gift to the caricaturists and cartoonists, whereas with the person whose inner life has evolved, I think it is very hard to do a drawing-room imitation.

P. Yes, because they are not *fixed*.

P.B. So that in that sense, one could say, when one talks about our masks, what one really means is our rigidities. Somebody who has got just two expressions is someone whose natural capacity for being all the time in motion has become sclerosed, rigidified. Even someone who has twenty or even a thousand expressions—that is still not a lot, compared with the life force; it is still limited.

P. What about the mask maker? It seems important, what is invested in the creation of the form. There is a link that exists between the maker and the wearer.

P.B. These two actions traditionally are considered sacred actions. There is something that is understood as demanding respect in both operations. There are little rituals that are performed before putting on a mask or beginning to carve one, different things like sprinkling water or touching the ground, that show that it is more than a simple artisanal process. But in Western theater, I think it is a terrible thing almost always, the use of masks designed by painters and artists; because what do modern designers actually imagine that they are working *from*? They are making a face—but from what? That is a question that is by-passed. From what, and with what, are they making a face? It is not surprising that the result is neither flesh nor fowl, unless a person can stay very clearly in front of that question.

7

◆

An Interview with
Pauline de Dampierre

"The Seven Deadly Sins," VOL. X:4, November, 1985

The Human Place

*M*uch has been written about a certain spot in Paris where *a kind of inner fire was kept burning throughout the dark days and nights of the German occupation. In a small and crowded apartment in the rue des Colonels Renard, a strangely assorted group of people met nightly to listen with absorbed attention to an Armenian Greek named Gurdjieff, to eat the amazing meals he cooked for them, and to hear read aloud the still-unpublished* Beelzebub's Tales to His Grandson.

Pauline de Dampierre was one of the circle. She was a young attorney who turned journalist after the war was over; but like many another of the gifted young, she was not destined to follow either of the careers she had originally chosen for herself. Her meeting with Gurdjieff was definitive. After it, her professional work continued only as a means for living and a ground for self-study. After Gurdjieff's death in 1949 and until the present, she has continued, in company with others of that same circle, the process of work on his teaching, for herself, and with the many new people who have come asking to know more about the enigmatic Master and the ideas he expressed.

◆

PARABOLA I have been very much interested in the definition at the end of the introduction to Gurdjieff's book, *Meetings with Remarkable Men.* He

89

says, "He can be called a remarkable man who stands out from those around him by the resourcefulness of his mind, and who knows how to be restrained in the manifestations which proceed from his nature, at the same time conducting himself justly and tolerantly towards the weaknesses of others."

PAULINE DE DAMPIERRE Yes. He can be *just* in front of the weakness of the other, because by having learned to contain his own manifestation, he knows what he is; and he knows what the difficulty is. There is a Zen story that I think illustrates this very well. A blind man was listening to a conversation going on near him, and suddenly he cried out: "Oh, what an extraordinary man! I have never heard anything like it!" When he was asked what he had heard that was so remarkable, he explained: "You know that blind people always develop a very fine sense of hearing. Now, in my entire life, I have never heard someone congratulate another for some good fortune without hearing in his voice at the same time a note of jealousy; and I have never heard anyone sympathize with a misfortune without hearing in his voice a shade of superiority or of satisfaction because he himself was spared. But in the voice of this man who just spoke, when he spoke of happiness I heard only happiness, and when he expressed sorrow, I heard nothing but sorrow. . . . "

The man he had listened to was in fact a monk, a great Buddhist saint. Maybe you could say he was a "whole man."

But I don't mean by this to say that only people who reach this degree should be called "real"; because between the fully realized man who has attained the greatest development possible, and the ordinary contemporary man— "a slave entirely at the disposal of tendencies which have nothing to do with his true individuality"—there is room for another category of mankind: those who search for a way toward truth. In other words, one might say that these are people who have discovered a truth in the words of the blind man that goes far beyond a mere clever observation, which concerns them very deeply. They have seen that these almost unconscious states of feeling into which they let themselves fall are just one aspect of a much more serious problem—a fundamental problem, basic to their whole life. So they have decided to put everything they have into confronting it.

P. How do you feel the "whole man" relates to the idea of sin?

P. de D. What interests me is what is at the source of what we call sin. Usually we see sin as a manifestation of a certain intensity, or as an action which is exaggerated, bad, harmful. But what is at the source of that action? Compared to the source, the action is only an excrescence— something that bursts through from an undercurrent which is always acting in human beings.

The undercurrent of tendencies from which these impulses arise is a part of the whole man.

P. These are motivating forces?

P. de D. Usually these tendencies have a much greater influence on our behavior than we imagine. They are always moving, and they are at the root of what has been called our automatism. If a person were to stop all his outer and inner movements at a given moment in order to see what is acting in him, he would nearly always feel a tendency which has about it something narrow, something heavy, something with a negative aspect that tends to be against, to be egoistic. All that is usually going on unseen. But if he tries to awaken to what is going on in himself, to be sincere, he will be able to witness, in addition to what could be called the "coarse" life in him, another life of another quality—much subtler, much higher, lighter—that is also a part of himself. The contact with this other quality of life helps him to have a quieter presence, a deeper vision. And he feels an urge at that moment to be open to a quality of this sort that would have a force, that would be a center of gravity. He begins to search for a way to serve what he feels would be his real being.

Then he begins to really know that if he lets his attention, his interest, be taken by his automatic tendencies, it deprives him of contact with that other source of life he is searching for. It could be said that there is a continual tendency to sin, in that sense. When these sins are spoken of as deadly, it means that these tendencies—if they are allowed to rule—at every moment deprive the human being of the possibility of turning towards this real life.

P. When you speak of this undercurrent, do you mean the passive?

P. de D. Passive. . . . To let oneself be continuously led by these automatic, nonconscious tendencies is indeed to be passive. And when a person is passive, the automatic begins to take the initiative, to direct him. When he turns towards something else. . . .

P. When he makes a contact between the two?

P. de D. Yes, then the undercurrent is able to play its normal role—its very necessary role.

P. Without a search, is there any sin? Is there responsibility without an aim?

P. de D. It is often said that man in his state of illusion about himself is not responsible, and perhaps in that sense it could be said that there is no sin. But to what extent is he absolutely not responsible?

P. Is he held responsible at some level?

P. de D. What we know is that every time we let ourselves go strongly into one of these tendencies, the tendency is strengthened. After a time it becomes very difficult to be free of it. It is in that way I see that one pays for his actions. And what about the harm that has been done to others through us? It is a very serious question.

P. I'm interested in what you say about these tendencies being natural. If they are natural tendencies, always there as an undercurrent, what are they there for? And what is the difference when they are there as an undercurrent and when they are acted out? Do they become sins only when they are expressed?

P. de D. One can feel these tendencies as inescapable parts of one's nature which to a certain extent bring data about oneself and the external world. I have to sustain my life. Many demands come to me from external life and I must sustain my outer life with the ego—as I am, I have nothing else. So it is through these tendencies that the ego is informed.

Take anger, for example. With a little vigilance, it is possible at the beginning of a movement of anger to surprise in oneself the sudden, sharp upsurge of an instinctive impulse that tends to immediately reject whatever is irritating us, making us suffer. This impulse is necessary—how could we get along without it? We would be inert—we could let our hand stay in a fire without reacting.

Take envy. There exists a law according to which when two masses of unequal size are near one another, the larger provokes a tension in the smaller. I should add that I know nothing about physics and do not know if this law prevails in that domain. But it is indubitably among the psychic influences that act on us, whether we like it or not. Very probably it is thanks to this law that the child instinctively educates itself, seeking to imitate an older person. He admires him, wants to be like him, wants to draw his attention, and if he doesn't succeed in doing so, he is frightened. For adults, it is exactly the same.

And pride—don't we teach a child to be proud of his successes, of his strength? Lacking this pride, he wouldn't respect himself and wouldn't make himself respected by others.

In a way each one of these tendencies is there to sustain my life at a certain level; they are necessary and healthy. But if I live with them alone, I am an animal. A human being has to stand in between and not allow himself to be taken by these things; not to let them raise opposition and justification. For this he must not let himself identify with them, and this means he must not let them make him forget the one and only thing important for him.

P. These sins, then, are engines of the ego? They drive the ego?

P. de D. I would even say that they are engines of our nature, because we can always find these tendencies acting in us. But if one can see them, one can be informed by them instead of being blindly taken.

You were speaking of the ego. . . . On the portals of certain cathedrals, one can see sculptures representing the vices and, above them, sculptures of the virtues. But between the vices and the virtues, there is something intermediary. And this is not shown. In fact, what remains hidden in the middle is man's wish to be sincere, to try to understand the meaning of his life. But for this, the underlying current must be perceived, and respected. Then the virtues take on form on their own. It isn't necessary to seek them directly. They appear.

The rest of the time, it is ego speaking. There is no other alternative.

These virtues do not judge, do not reject, have no violence. They emanate; they radiate. Certain exceptional human beings prove that this is so, and even in someone who is very far from that, the existence of such a possibility can make itself felt.

P. In a way, it is like saying that only a person who knows fear can be courageous. There is no need of virtue if you don't have vices!

P. de D. What is vice? There are many ways to look at the subject—psychologically, analytically, theologically. I have no intention of adding to what has already been said along these lines. I simply want to emphasize one aspect that is rarely brought to light: the role of an inner search in relation to these underlying tendencies. Then the "vices" become simpler. You don't so much think of them as bad, but you feel strongly, painfully, that they are harmful to what you are searching for. They are there and you don't allow them to take too much place. You don't reject them, but you don't let yourself be engulfed by them, either. Through this process, something can be developed in us.

P. That brings a note of hope—and it bears on our earlier question about *why* the undercurrent is there.

P. de D. What is important is to begin to be able to hold oneself at the source. I heard during my Catholic upbringing that even a saint sinned seven times a day. But I would say that the tendency to sin is at every second.

P. And it is not one's fault that it is there?

P. de D. It is my human place. The power to act is in the body. The wish for evolved being comes from another source. And the two parts must meet. They do not often meet by accident; they meet only when something is acknowledged and held in respect.

P. These impulses, then, if held at the source, can actually contribute to a continued sense of presence?

P. de D. My sense of presence will only be real if I take these impulses into account. I may try to open only to something higher—perhaps it is possible in a posture of meditation, but even then not so easy. But the moment I begin to act these impulses are necessarily there, and must be taken into account.

P. Unquestionably, they have enormous force. It seems that something else of an equal force needs to be there. One can be aware of one of these impulses for a moment, and suddenly be swallowed by it. And then it is the only thing there.

P. de D. I would say that what is needed is not an equal force but another kind of force, more subtle, more active. As in chemistry, one can take a stone and introduce a very active substance and the stone will dissolve. Well, the wish to be can be very active.

In fact it is not possible to experience an opening towards more freedom without obedience toward something higher. A human being has no other possibility. He may think he can be free, but he is either obedient and submitting to this higher, or a slave. But when he submits willingly, he may receive something of such a high quality that he will no longer be attracted to what enslaves him. Every time we are attracted, we think we find life in that attraction. But at the moment of submitting to this finer force, we feel life of such another kind that we are no longer tempted.

There is a very strong relation between the action of these tendencies and a certain automatism of the body. Of course, we all know how easily tempted we are by physical satisfactions—resting, moving about, food, sexual attraction. But what I'm speaking of is much more hidden, insidious, almost beyond uprooting by ordinary means. It's a question of a certain "coarseness" inscribed in the body by everything that we have experienced, by the way in which we have allowed ourselves to be led along by these impulses. The body is accustomed to this heavy functioning even if outwardly it seems extremely light and free. The very texture of the body favors these impulses and is reinforced by them. It's a vicious circle. When there is an opening to something higher, the body quietens, and begins to be impregnated with something more subtle. It finds a kind of inner behavior much more in accordance with this opening. And in that way these tendencies begin not to have such a strong action on the person.

P. What is the place of feeling, here? Does feeling have no action at all? Is this a struggle only between the head and body?

P. de D. It is said that we have almost no contact with real feeling. Our emotions are very egoistic. There is no love in them. They always turn me to something other than what is there. When we feel emotions, there is a vibration so quick and tempting that it is difficult to resist. We always think it is our feeling, but it is not our feeling—it is our emotionality. If you observe yourself at that moment, you will recognize that that emotion is not yourself. You have no liberty; you are absolutely engulfed. Yet there is this mysterious power in the human being—to turn also towards something else in himself that may be very weak, nearly inaudible, but of another quality that he respects more. One could say that real feeling appears at those rare moments when what is happening in the individual is of such quality that his only wish is to be able to remain there, and to serve it as best he can. It is only then that he has a positive feeling of the moment, with no wish to be somewhere else.

P. There seems to be a sense in which the impulses of envy, avarice, and so on seem to have to do with the future or the past—with images of something that I want, and fear that I will not be able to have. I am taken out of the present moment by wanting to insure something for the future. Do you think these impulses are based on fear?

P. de D. In our usual state, we have nothing real in us to rely on, so it is necessary for us to create projections and ideas, to have desires of all kinds. We have no aim that would feed our presence. Every real search is about that—to find a place in oneself one could serve, where being could grow and play its role. Then it gives sense to life. When it appears, true relationship begins among the parts of the individual. One sees better, one is clearer at that moment, one is no longer afraid of living. Even outwardly, something is more balanced. Without that, there is never an aim which brings me in contact with the sense of my destiny. But at that moment, no matter how briefly, I see that I am in contact with the aim that I've sought. I know what to place my confidence in.

P. We are almost forced, then, to imagine some kind of reality for ourselves, because we are not in touch with a true reality. We have to create some sort of world to live in.

P. de D. I would say that we haven't been taught that we could be open to the growth of a reality in us. It is a great discovery to touch something real and tangible in us—it is the goal of all the traditions, to help the individual toward what is real in him.

P. There is very little in our society that lends support to a search of this kind. Why should anyone believe you when you say that something more is possible for human beings?

P. de D. These ideas seem quite alien, it's true. Today, however, several great currents of spiritual search are trying to give them new reality.

For my part, I would say that one of the most remarkable aspects of Gurdjieff's thought is that it allows us to start from where we are—from our mortal sins, one might say, or more simply from our predominant faults. It casts a vigorous, surprising, light of truth on our multiple weaknesses, our prison. And it shows us how to listen to another voice, enter into contact with another reality.

How to be touched? One can be deeply touched by contact with someone who has begun to develop this in himself. Or special events can happen in life—a great happiness, a great sorrow, an impression of nature, of sacred art of the past—that can give an extraordinary feeling of much more life in us, much finer, much broader, as if the horizon were opening.

It gives us a taste that life should always be like that. It doesn't happen often and it comes through events outside of us. But the longing for it is always there. For we are speaking of a human need—the need that makes us alive.

To feel it is to feel that it is true and must be searched for.

A real search is a preparation for an opening to the taste of that life. Gaining knowledge of everything that opposes it is the first step on the path. And it is a great adventure. . . .

8

◆

An Interview with
Brother David Steindl-Rast
by John Loudon

"Holy War," VOL. VII:4, October, 1982

Becoming What You Are

To those who encounter Brother David now and again, he seems very much a man on the move, remarkably mobile for a monk. Yet despite all this traveling and speaking, he always appears a calm eye at the center of any storm of activity. To a passing observer, he might look disturbingly gaunt and ascetic, confirming popular prejudices about monks being world-haters. But as soon as he greets you, the illusion of severity vanishes: he is so warm and effervescent that you really want to learn how he packs so much alertness and delight into his life.

Born in Vienna, Brother David has a doctorate in psychology and has been a monk for thirty years. He says that he is as much at home in a Zen monastery as in a Catholic one, and it's hard to think that he would not be at home anywhere. For he has a remarkable ability to be joyfully and wholly present: when he listens, he does nothing else; when the phone interrupts, he takes the call with full attention and delight; when he answers questions he does so with the kind of care and élan that make an interviewer's task a joy. More than many teachers, the man is his message, and it is hard to imagine a more persuasive and attractive advocate for the Catholic monastic tradition.

Many people ask him whether the spirituality he embodies and presents is really the Catholicism that they've found so difficult to appreciate in other forms which they've encountered. But it may be that few people have so appropriated that tradition that they can express it with such simple grace.

John Loudon, PARABOLA's first editor, became Editor of Religious Books for

Harper & Row in San Francisco in 1977. He is presently senior partner of Co-Venture Associates, Inc., a publishing services company.

◆

JOHN LOUDON: What does "holy warfare" mean to you?

BROTHER DAVID STEINDL-RAST: Today the notion of warfare is inseparable from that of alienation, whereas the very essence of spiritual warfare in the monastic tradition is the overcoming of alienation—what we call nowadays pulling or getting yourself together. And the monastic symbol for pulling yourself together is the belt, which monks wear in many different traditions. The aim is to overcome alienation from yourself, from others, and from God.

J.L. What forces need to be overcome in this struggle against alienation?

B.D. Well, in the classical discussion of holy warfare in the writings of the Eastern Fathers of the early church, these forces are personified as demons. Even in the New Testament Paul says that it is not against "flesh and blood" that we are struggling, but against principalities and powers of evil. But it's not necessary to take these powers literally, in a fundamentalist way, and in fact to do so we probably would do an injustice to the early Fathers who wrote in those terms. They were no doubt as alert to the metaphorical nature of this imagery as we are, just as Buddhists have long known that the different hells in their tradition are best understood as mental or psychological states, not actual places.

J.L. Can you give examples of some of these personified forces and some indication of how you might express them today?

B.D. The three great forces that the Latin Fathers identified as the enemies against which we're battling are anger, lust, and laziness. The third one is called the noonday devil. It is in the middle of everything—of a day, of a life—that you can lose your resolve, that torpor can set in. When you're in the middle of swimming across a river, it's too far to go back and seems too far to reach the other side, and you are tempted to give up. Well, these three elements—anger, lust, and laziness—are precisely the three ways that we can fail to be present where we are, and the whole idea of getting yourself together is to be present where you are and, in the Christian context, to respond to the presence of God.

Anger really means impatience (as opposed to the righteous anger that is desirable in many circumstances). Impatience makes us get ahead of ourselves, reaching out for something in the future and not really being content with where we are, here and now.

Lust extends much wider than the sexual sphere, and essentially means attachment, attachment to something that is not present, or is not the appropriate thing right now.

And one by-product of laziness, of being victimized by the noonday devil, is sadness—not the genuine sorrow of compassion, but the lifeless *ennui* of never really being involved in the present, with what's happening.

If you would like another contemporary interpretation of the idea of spiritual warfare, there is C.S. Lewis's *The Screwtape Letters*, in which he translates the tradition with great wit and insight into a modern idiom. It's all about struggling with the forces that are all around us in the world and within us and that distract us from being really unified, in one piece.

J.L. When I was thinking about the theme of holy warfare, it occurred to me that there are military virtues—such as discipline, strength, courage, resolve, fidelity, and so on—which are also vital to spiritual growth. And especially the aspect of discipline, involving training and regular practice. What are the disciplines that have been developed that can be used against these devils today?

B.D. The word discipline is very significant in this context, since it is not primarily a military term. The corresponding military term is regimentation. Discipline is a school term: the *discipulus* is the disciple, the pupil. Even the word pupil is apt here, because it is related to the pupil in our eye, the *pupilla*—the little doll, the little image of oneself that one sees in another's eye. This eye-to-eye contact is the essence of discipline: discipline is the attitude that you have when you see eye-to-eye with your teacher. Today especially people reject external regimentation, and are looking for a teacher that gives discipline eye-to-eye. The drill sergeant doesn't care if you are eye-to-eye with him or anybody else, just that you do what you are told. But discipline involves bringing out what is already within you. That's what the true teacher does. And the other virtues you mentioned have similar parallels. Fortitude or courage, for instance, is simply the resolve to overcome obstacles. Spiritual warfare involves the acquiring and implementation of the strengths and virtues needed to overcome obstacles.

J.L. Discipline suggests to me habits of behavior and regular practices that the teacher would presumably teach. How does this dimension relate to overcoming anger, lust, laziness?

B.D. Within the monastery, which is my background and the essential environment that I feel comfortable with and know well, there is a particularly highly developed tradition of such training. In fact, the monastery can be understood precisely as a setting in which this discipline is cultivated. It is a place to which people go in order to get themselves together, again in the sense of uniting with themselves, with others, with God.

The two realms in which this discipline is cultivated are space and time, and the aim is that the whole of life should be brought together from alienation to fullness. With regard to time, for instance, there are in monasteries all sort of bells, gongs, clappers, drums, and so on—all kinds of signals that tell you what it is time for. The struggle is within yourself to overcome your laziness, your attachments, your impatience in order to be truly wherever you need to be at any particular time. T.S. Eliot speaks of "Time, not our time," and he explicitly says this in relation to the Angelus bell that, in monastic life, rings three times a day—at sunrise, at sunset, and at high noon. The sun doesn't rise again or wait for you if you oversleep and don't get up when the bell rings. The sun rises and the bell rings, and you are to be there: your impatience can't make it happen before the right time; your attachment to staying in bed can't delay it; and you'll miss it if you're up but not really present, alert, attentive. If this sort of timeliness appeals to you, as it does to me, these signals are not a torturing regimentation but musical invitations, celebrations of particular moments.

The difficult aspect, of course, is the one expressed by St. Benedict in his

Rule: "When the bell rings, stop everything. Don't even cross your t's or dot your i's, but go quickly." The challenge is to learn to respond immediately to whatever it is time for. Not to wonder whether you have time for it or whether you like it, but simply to respond when it is time. And the truth of this discipline is universal. For instance, in Taoism, the flow goes on and you can either be in tune with the flow or not. All these signals are simply means to get you into the flow, and the less you are in tune the more difficult the immediate responding is, the more obstacles you have to overcome to get with it.

With regard to space, the monastery is organized in such a way that there is a place for everything, and relatedly that everything is there, the monastery is self-contained. The ideal is wonderfully expressed in the Benedictine tradition by the famous plan of St. Gall, which is reflected more or less in many medieval monasteries. With everything there and a place for everything, you can be at home in your world, in the place where you belong. And belonging and getting yourself together are closely related. This sufficient world, which St. Benedict calls a workshop for the spiritual life, affords the spaces and the tools for working on yourself, transforming yourself, and in turn the world around you.

Novices always have difficulties with both aspects—time and space. When it is time for something, they often want to do something else; when this is the place to be, they often want to be somewhere else. And isn't this how it is for most people? The monastery also emphasizes neatness and orderliness; most visitors notice this immediately. There is a close relation between the struggle to put things in order within yourself, within your life, and the ordering of the space around you. But novices find this hard to understand. They say, "We came here to learn spiritual matters, and what I'm told to do is how to put my shoes on, when to put them on and take them off, to put them down with the right one on the right side, the left on the left, and parallel, not toed in. What does that have to do with the spiritual life?" It has everything to do with it. That is the spirituality; it isn't something that you do just as a novice, and then graduate to spirituality. But it takes a long time to see that orderliness and cleanliness is not just cleaning the room, but it is getting your life in order.

So bringing things into order is the goal. Order is the disposition of things in which each gives to the other its room, its own proper place.

That's the external aspect. The other is that order that springs from love: there's no other way of establishing order except through love. So spiritual warfare is radically unlike what we know as warfare, which is rooted in hate and alienation and leads to chaos.

J.L. Besides the imagery of warfare, some people have compared spiritual discipline to athletic training. There is the talk, for instance, about becoming an athlete of Christ.

B.D. Both the athletic imagery and that of spiritual weaponry occur in St. Paul, but the weapons he speaks of are faith, hope, and love. I am convinced that in the present world, in which peace and order are no longer possible through arms, it is best to change our spiritual vocabulary, because misunderstandings do arise on the popular level. I am much more comfortable with speaking about spiritual struggle, since that does not necessarily involve struggling against someone else. You can struggle up a mountain, or struggle to get your body in shape. It even applies to animals: a chick struggling to get out of the eggshell. Plants struggle to break through cracks in the concrete, and amazingly they manage to. And similarly, I prefer to speak of obstacles rather than enemies. *The struggle against obstacles*, I think, puts the essentials of the tradition of spiritual warfare into contemporary language that is proper and helpful.

J.L. Do you think the spiritual path demands a special way of life?

B.D. If by a special way of life, you mean a special place like a monastery, I would say no. But if the question implies making an effort, having to struggle, I would say yes. The difference between other animals around us and ourselves seems to be that dogs and cats and birds and other animals don't have to struggle to be good at what they are. But we human beings somehow have to struggle to become what we are.

J.L. Our being is to become.

B.D. Yes. We experience ourselves as unfinished, and we have to struggle to become a finished product. Actually, we're never completely finished; that's our glory and our agony. We remain open-ended.

J.L. In contemporary Catholicism, and in the past as well, there seem to be two divergent paths: there is that of those who emphasize spirituality, spiritual disciplines and growth, and then there is the more general, popular path in which salvation is available through regular participation in the sacraments and the life of the church generally. The former way sees *becoming* a Christian as a lifelong task; the latter stresses fidelity to *being* a good Catholic. Can you say something about this?

B.D. You speak of participating in the sacraments. At the heart of all the sacraments, especially the eucharist and baptism, is the celebration of the struggle of Christ through death to resurrection. If you really participate in the sacrament, it is impossible not to enter into that struggle. The whole idea of the sacrament is to go through that struggle yourself in communion with the struggle of Christ, to participate day by day and hour by hour in the struggle of dying into greater fullness of life. And the real issue is not whether there is one kind of life that allows for this acceptance of death that leads to fuller life, and so is a spiritual life rather than a run-of-the-mill life. No, the real question is to what extent within ordinary life we can wake up to the essential inner struggle of realizing the fullness of life. Going to church, sending your kids to Catholic schools, and so on, by themselves don't do anything; they're worthless, unless they lead you into, wake you up to that struggle.

J.L. Since you participate in both the Christian and the Zen communities, do you think there is an ultimate difference between Chrisianity and Buddhism, and what kinds of differences do you see between the two?

B.D. The point is, how ultimate is "ultimate"? There are many different levels. On one level there are great cultural differences: the two traditions grew up in entirely different settings, and so are dissimilar in many respects. But the moment that you penetrate through the accidental cultural differences, you find a remarkable similarity. Sometimes now I cannot remember if I'm in a Christian or a Buddhist monastery. The atmosphere is very similar. Then you go deeper still, and you discover profound differences in approach, although it's difficult to put them into words. Basically, the Biblical tradition centers on the Word in the widest sense: the divine speaks to us, approaches us, and we have to respond; we're burdened with *responsibility*.

J.L. The Bible also emphasizes hearing over seeing.

B.D. And the reason for the emphasis on hearing is the call to live by the word of God, being nourished by it, responding to it. In Zen the stress is not on the word, but on the silence—the silence that is so profound that you can go down into it forever and ever. Openness, emptiness, void—all this permeates Zen. Of course, in the Christian tradition, the Word comes out of the silence and returns to the silence. But despite the teaching of the dark night of the soul and the like, the Christian tradition still stays very close to the Word. Though there are lots of words in Buddhism, they aim at silence. After everything is said and done, the Zen teacher will say, "Ah yes, but what a pity that we have to say anything at all." The saying doesn't really effect anything; what counts is the silence of practice. But then, if you go still deeper down, to what I think might well be the deepest level, you can experience communion and unity between the traditions, the complementarity of the Word and the silence.

J.L. What is the connection between the life of contemplation and the call to social action in the world?

B.D. You can't really be a contemplative, unless you also want to change the world. You want to change yourself, and that's where the struggle comes in. By changing yourself, you're beginning to change the world. In fact, you're changing the world much more by changing yourself than if you're running around blindly, involved in one cause after another. But the difference between what we call the apostolic and the contemplative orders, or vocations, is that the apostolic approach says, "We live in this world, we're responsible for it, and we have to do something to change the world for the better." The monastic answer is, "We are not strong enough to change the world in general. Let's change that little spot where we are. And let's put a wall around it and say this is as far as we go, as far as our strength reaches. And now within that narrow confine, let's change the world, make it more what it's supposed to be." That approach has its drawbacks, too, because it can become ingrown, its own private little affair. And the apostolic approach has limitations, because it can become so watered down that nothing spiritual remains. So we need the two; they are the poles of one continuum. People who are now engaged in apostolically changing the world need to come back periodically to a monastic environment where what they are trying to achieve everywhere is to a certain extent achieved already. And if the world could gradually become what a good monastery or Zen center is, that would be fine. The monastic communities can provid the strength, the encouragement to realize that true order can be achieved.

J.L. Traditionally, Catholicism has emphasized that the contemplative life is valuable in and of itself, even if the effect on the outside world is not very immediate or direct, but with the faith that spiritual service of God would redound ultimately to the benefit of mankind. How would you translate that idea into contemporary terms?

B.D. The problem is that all too easily you can think of the spiritual as the opposite of the material. But in authentic Christianity, the material is completely integrated with the spiritual. The essence of Christianity is incarnation. Spiritual is not opposed to material, but to the unspiritual. It's better to speak of alive and dead. Spirit, "breath," means life. The unspiritual or "the flesh," as the New Testament puts it, does not mean the material, the bodily. Flesh stands for that which is dead and in the process of decay. So it's best to think of death not in the sense of negating life, denying life. Life-affirming and life-denying are what spiritual and unspiritual mean. So from that viewpont, there is a struggle for more and more spirituality, but this spirituality does not deny the world and material things, but expresses itself in more and more beautiful transformation of the material world. Now and then you see a place where every roof tile and every door knob speaks of spirituality, and it reminds you that material things can be completely transformed.

J.L. I asked you earlier if a spiritual life demanded a special way of life, and in the light of the distinctions that you've made, I'm beginning to think that what it actually comes down to concretely is how you spend your day. Of course, monks spend their day differently than people who drive trucks or work in offices and so on. How do you spend your day? And what principles that the monastic life has taught you might apply to people who live in the "ordinary world"?

B.D. The challenge of living according to certain principles is the same for everyone, and we all need to live a special kind of life if we want to come truly alive. The monastic day starts with getting up earlier than most would like to get up. So the struggle is right there at the start.

J.L. Do you get up earlier because it is difficult, or because it's good to be up when the sun comes up?

B.D. You never do anything, theoretically or ideally, just because it's more difficult. You do it in spite of its being difficult, but for a good reason. The reason for getting up early is that these early morning hours provide a setting, a quiet, a silence that never comes again later in the day; there is something special going on in those early hours. And you're also there for the sunrise, dawn, which is very important: you celebrate the dawning of each new day. But it's a struggle to get up and to remain alert.

Then during the day, there are several times for prayer and times when we get together to celebrate important points in the day—high noon, sunset, night prayers at the end of the day. The rest of the time is spent studying or in manual labor. Manual labor is significant and everybody in the monastery takes part in it, including the abbot. It's simply a part of life. It keeps you humble, down to earth (*humus*—the word that also gives us humor and human). Essentially, then, monastic life is dedicated to prayer, manual labor, and study.

J.L. How much of this regimen can you take with you when you travel?

B.D. It's very difficult, and that's why monks don't usually travel. The kind of prayer that I find most helpful, in place of the divine office that is chanted several times a day in the monastery, is the prayer of the heart from the Eastern Christian tradition, which involves a kind of mantric repetition of the name of Jesus. But I try to restrict my travel, because it's so hard to take much of the monastery with you, although it's fine if I can stay in another monastery, such as Zen or Camaldolese [one of the Benedictine orders in the Roman Catholic church with a monastery in southern California].

J.L. And how would you suggest that the values of that sort of structure be translated to people who live their whole lives in the situation you find yourself in when you're not in the monastery?

B.D. There's no point in just imitating the externals. What one should and can take out of the monastic life is its very essence, and that is the grateful approach to life moment by moment, being grateful in everything you do. That means, for instance, an alertness to the character of every moment as a given moment, a gift. Every moment demands a response, and the basic Christian response is trust in the giver.

J.L. But you can't have awareness just by wanting it, can you? There are people here at the Zen Center who have spent years and years of their lives trying to be more awake.

B.D. That's true. But there are degrees of wakefulness. And people who have practiced for years and years may not realize that they have made great steps toward greater wakefulness. The difficulty in speaking about wakefulness is that when you are asleep you can't just wake yourself up. But if you focus on thankfulness, it is easier, since being grateful is within your power. If you do it again and again, you remind yourself that every moment is a given moment. Gratefulness is an experience that everyone has, and seems very natural when cultivated. Actually, it is emphasized more explicitly in Buddhist monasteries, where there are so many formal bows. It is a form of teaching us to receive everything—a cup of tea, another person—with gratitude.

J.L. So this rhythm of gift and response is a spiritual practice, or at least a way that anybody can practice in any circumstances.

B.D. Yes, and I don't think spiritual practice is too grandiose a term for it. If you really explore its larger implications, it is at the core of every spiritual practice, although it may be expressed in quite different ways.

J.L. What is the importance of the dialogue between Christianity and Zen?

B.D. These are traditions that seem to me to have a lot of future and that complement one another well. And what really interested me in Buddhist-Christian dialogue was the monastic dimension. I wanted to know in what sense Buddhists are monks like I am. And ultimately I've come to see that the monastic life isn't something that is especially connected to Buddhism or to Christianity, but is related to one's frame of mind, one's own inner bent.

J.L. So it's an essential human vocation or option; in any culture or society there are going to be people who want to live this way?

B.D. Right, and you could even think of it as an externalization of a dimension that is in every human being and is sometimes very strong in people who do not externalize it because of their life circumstances.

J.L. You spoke about our always becoming and never reaching the end. What is it that one is supposed to become? What's the struggle for?

B.D. As the Christian tradition sees it, each one of us is a unique word that is spoken, or a unique way of saying the one eternal Word of God. Each one of us is a word, and we become the word that we are by our response to all the other words around us, human or otherwise. Thus we become the word that we are meant to be. If the word is in the process of being spoken, you can never really say it's finished. In a certain sense, the word is completed with my death, when all that I have made of my life is rounded off. But even then, the Cappadocian Fathers in the early church taught that heaven is not a static state, but a dynamic experience of moving deeper and deeper into the ultimate, and the ultimate can never be completely discovered.

J.L. If you're playing tennis, I suppose that one person eventually wins in the end, but the joy of playing is not just getting to the end. But what about the people who aren't even playing the game?

B.D. I tend to believe that even in people in whom we least see it, deep down there is that aliveness, that longing, that struggle, and it's just well covered over. My world view is not that there are a few people who really struggle and that the masses haven't awakened to their real calling. My view is that in some the process is more obvious and in others the process is more hidden. And that is a common view in monastic traditions, East and West. Both have stories of the spiritual master who is very accomplished and is having trouble finding a teacher of his own. And he is directed, in a dream or a vision or in some other way, to someone who is more advanced than he is, but is the last person you would have expected. In Buddhism it's a butcher for example, someone way down the spiritual line, whom you'd expect to have no spiritual consciousness at all. And in the Christian tradition it's often a merchant with a big family and no time to pray, just buying and selling all day. And all of a sudden the searching teacher discovers this is it, this is the one.

And the most urgent spiritual task today is one being waged by just such "ordinary people"—the struggle against nuclear arms, the struggle for peace, which means harmony among all things.

J.L. What do you regard as your special vocation?

B.D. These days I'm more and more involved in working with people who are quite alienated from the Christian tradition, even though many of them were raised as Christians. I very much enjoy, for instance, workshops with New Age people, many of whom come out of a Christian background but have been away from it for a long time and are now ready to give Christianity a new look. Essentially, my vocation is simply to be a monk, but part of that is this sort of healing mission that not too many others are involved in.

J.L. So your vocation is to live the Christian monastic life, and then to communicate what you discover in it?

B.D. Really the latter part is more a matter of exposing myself to other people who have the monk within them, and haven't discovered it. One doesn't need to say much; it seems to be a help to find a monk who can be a catalyst for the monastic bent of mind that is in all of us.

9

♦

An Interview with
Isaac Bashevis Singer

"Demons," VOL. VI:4, October, 1981

Demons by Choice

*I**saac** Bashevis Singer came to the United States from his native Poland in 1939. From that time to this, virtually everything he writes first appears in story or serialized form in Yiddish in the* Jewish Daily Forward. *He has written some eight novels from* The Manor *and* The Family Moskat *to* Shosha *and* Old Love; *endless short stories from* A Friend of Kafka *to* A Crown of Feathers; *books for children—*The Fools of Chelm, Why Noah Chose the Dove, Naftali the Storyteller and His Horse, Sus, *and autobiographical works:* In My Father's Court *and two volumes of his autobiography,* A Young Man in Search of Love *and* Lost in America. *He has been unstintingly generous with his time and energy—talking to everyone about everything—sharing the stories. Until he won the Nobel Prize for Literature in 1978, which brought with it recognition and unbelievable demands, Singer was one of the very few authors who was listed in the New York phone book or who answered his own phone. He continues to be a visible part of New York's West Side—strolling the streets, or eating in one or another of his favorite neighborhood restaurants.*

We spoke to him in New York in the midst of a 95-degree heat wave. He had just finished an exhausting lecture tour and a series of book-signings. But he gave of himself once more, and elected to talk about demons because, he said, "the subject interests me."

Does Singer believe in the devil? Do demons exist as a separate reality? After reading the novels, the stories, the memoirs, after talking with the man himself, one is left with what may be the greatest gift of the very great storyteller: a richly-

117

etched, deeply-felt portrait of our condition; no easy answers; and questions that enrich us and actively engage us in a search that Singer himself pursues with such benefit to us all.

◆

PARABOLA Do you think we need demons?

ISAAC BASHEVIS SINGER Do you mean do we need them in life?

P. Yes.

I.B.S. It's a good question. I think it would be necessary. Because if people would never see anything of the supernatural, if we would never have any contact with other entities, we would live out our life with the feeling that this is it: our so-called reality is the only thing which exists. And that would make the human spirit much smaller than it is.

P. Do you feel that the demons we deal with are as you say in *Gimpel the Fool* like "shoulders and burdens" from God?

I.B.S. If they exist, they certainly are from God. There is nothing in the universe which is not from God. If a person believes in nature, everything is from nature, which is again everything. There is a unity in the creation. We cannot believe in anything else.

P. But does everything have a dark side, an "other" side?

I.B.S. I think that everything might have God knows how many sides! We don't know ourselves how many. Because if you take a pebble, you can look at this pebble from a chemical point of view, from a gravitational point of view—from many other points of view. According to Spinoza, the number of attributes of God are endless. And even if you believe in nature, you can say the same thing: that this pebble still can be seen from very many points of view.

P. One of the things that seems very strong in your work is an idea that the "demons" are put here to test us. . . .

I.B.S. I would say that behind all my ideas, the strongest idea of mine which is conveyed in my thinking, even more than in my writing, is the freedom of choice. I feel that the freedom of choice is the very essence of life. Although the gifts which God has given us are small in comparison to the gifts which He has given maybe to the angels or to the stars, we have one great gift—and this is to choose. If we pay attention to a thing, we have chosen to pay attention to it. If we love somebody, we have chosen this person for love. This is in every act of humanity. To me, God is freedom. And nature, to me, is necessity. Everything in nature is necessity. In God—who I think can overrule nature, is above nature—everything is free.

P. But what about a situation like the one you describe in *Satan of Goray*? Would it make a difference if we acted differently? Or is it inevitable that we must encounter demons?

I.B.S. When people abandon free choice, the demons appear. The demons are in a way the dark side of nature which we choose. If we stop believing in our power, then other powers can come upon us. In other words, to me the demon is the negative side of free choice. But we have free choice in every minute of our day; we can always choose. Even if we have a bad choice to make, there is always one thing which is better than the other.

P. Can we be *easily* possessed by demons?

I.B.S. I don't think they can take us over so quickly. They only come when people resign from almost everything. When people say to themselves, "I'm not going to make any choices anymore. I will just let the powers work for themselves." It is then that the demon is bound to appear.

P. Do you think we are in a time similar to the one you painted in *Satan in Goray* where the Evil One is triumphing again?

I.B.S. I would say we are always in such a time. If not the whole of humanity . . . you look what's going on, let's say, in this country with crime: if you go to a court where there should be justice, there is the very opposite—people you can buy for money . . . I would say human life is in one big crisis. The moment you have conquered one crisis, there is already another one lurking.

I think it is a part of being alive, of choosing. In other words, the danger is always there: the danger of turning love into hatred, of turning justice into injustice, of turning talent into non-talent, and so on and so on. . . .

P. Do you think that your God would fight for us? Is God at war?

I.B.S. I will tell you: He doesn't fight for us. Since He gave us free choice, He gave us a great gift, and we have to use it or misuse it. In other words, when it comes to choosing, we must rely mostly on ourselves. In this respect Judaism is a little different from Christianity. Where the Christians believe that once you belong to the Christian religion, the powers are resolved: when Jesus died, all the others should be redeemed forever. We believe the opposite: that the crisis is always there, the danger is always there—like a medical doctor who will tell you that the microbes are always there in your mouth and in your stomach, and if you become weak, they begin to multiply and become very strong.

P. And if we lose our control, the microbes, or the demons, can take over.

I.B.S. Of course. Nothing which one man did, no matter how great he was, can really redeem you or guarantee you redemption forever.

P. And in your story, "The Mirror," it seems that you are suggesting that everyone has a demon in the mirror.

I.B.S. Of course. Just as we are medically surrounded by dangerous microbes, so our spirit has always to fight melancholy and disbelief and viciousness and cruelty and all kinds of things.

P. But in some of your stories, even in "Cunegunde," your demons have a kind of melancholy. . . .

I.B.S. Oh, but the very essence of demons is melancholy. Because it's the very opposite of hope.

P. So you have some sympathy. . . .

I.B.S. Of course, I have sympathy for everyone who suffers and lives. Because we are all living in a great, great struggle, whether we realize it or not. Sometimes we realize it. This is a very difficult thing—we very often say how difficult life is.

P. Do you think we learn from our encounters with the demons, facing those demons?

I.B.S. We learn all the time, even if we don't use all the time what we have learned—because just as we learn all the time, we also forget all the time. There is a permanent amnesia planted in us, which just as we keep on forgetting our dreams, we sometimes keep on forgetting our reality. You see a certain thing; you think you have learned. And then you make the same mistake again, which shows you didn't learn.

P. So, is there any hope for us?

I.B.S. I will tell you: we have to go through this kind of struggle. In a way, the hope is in the fact that life does not last forever; the crisis does not last, and behind all this crisis, behind all this darkness, there is a great light. We have to struggle, but we are not lost, because the powers that have created us are actually great and benign powers.

P. And you think we have the equipment to fight back?

I.B.S. We have the equipment. The only thing is we should not let it rust, we should not forget about it, we should not put it away, and say, where is it? We must be very much aware all the time—on the watch. This is true in science, it's true in literature. . . . If you don't all the time watch what you are doing, you're bound to make mistakes. In my own life, I feel it all the time. It's true in love, it's true in everything.

P. You don't really feel that "evil" is a separate force?

I.B.S. It's a part of what we call life. I don't think that the rocks have free choice, or the meteors. They live in the world of necessity—which is again a different kind of war. What can you call it? A higher war? But we are, so to say, soldiers. We have to fight.

Our life doesn't last forever. The moment we leave this world, the great struggle is over—at least for a time. In a way, death is not such a curse, but it's a time of resting. People are afraid of death because they were created so, to be afraid, because, if not, they would mishandle the body. Actually death is in a way a great resting after the struggle.

All the powers work so that you should come to a bad ending, but our soul works for the opposite—that the ending should be good. Actually, the ending is always good.

10

♦

An Interview with
Three Mohawk Chiefs

"Obstacles," VOL. V:4, August, 1980

Tom Porter

© Lee B. Ewing

Loran Thompson

© Lee B. Ewing

Jake Swamp

An Earthquake Coming

T*he Mohawks, Onondagas, Oneidas, Senecas, Cayugas, and Tuscaroras are the Six Nations of the Iroquois Confederacy. Iroquois society is based on a set of principles called The Great Law of Peace, which they have followed for hundreds of years and which was influential in the framing of our own Constitution. They are unique among Indian peoples in that their traditional Councils do not accept Federal funding; they continue to live on their own (much reduced and industrially damaged) lands and they claim the right to be considered a confederacy of sovereign nations.*

The Mohawks, like all Indian peoples after generations of "adaptation," are somewhat geographically scattered as well as ideologically divided. Famous for their skill as steel and bridge workers, the men take jobs all over the country, but for most their own land is Akwesasne—called by the United States and Canada the St. Regis and Six Nations reservations—which lies on both sides of the now dangerously polluted St. Lawrence River. Many nontraditionalists have accepted different forms of Christianity and are willing to cooperate with the governments of the "dominant culture," which in turn encourage their election of a Tribal Council which accepts Federal authority, and implement it with a Native police force. The traditional faction, or Longhouse people, who steadfastly maintain the old religion, the old ways and language of the people, and the principle of Mohawk sovereignty, and publish the Akwesasne Notes, a remarkable newspaper circulating among 100,000 readers, call these Tribal Councils "the elected people." The elective process, or decision by voting, is completely foreign to the traditional Iroquois way, where everything is settled by consensus, including the choosing of the Longhouse Council of Chiefs.

The division of the people among themselves between the "traditional" and the "elected" has been perhaps the worst and most painful difficulty the Mohawks have had to deal with, and it is striking evidence of their dedication to a central, sacred responsibility that their leaders have been able in the last few years to bring these differing factions together in a very hopeful coalition. The elected councils of both sides of the river are meeting with the Longhouse chiefs, and a pact has been made that all land claims, acquisitions, and disposals will be subject to their joint approval. It is urgent that new lands should be appropriated where the Mohawk people could live, farm, and fish, as Akwesasne's water and soil are now so poisoned that crops and cattle die, and water has to be hauled in for the children of the new Freedom School.

Five of us from PARABOLA's *staff spent a weekend with some of the Longhouse people at Raquette Point. Food there is sometimes in short supply, but they shared what they had with each other and with us. The strongest of many strong impressions that we had was of a quality of relationship and of mutual respect, between individuals and between men and women, that was, as Tom Porter says, so simple it was hard to comprehend. Here is the conversation we had with three truly remarkable men: Longhouse Chiefs Tom Porter, Loran Thompson, and Jake Swamp. We would be fortunate, and proud, to have such leaders. In the words of their extraordinary Law of Peace, "with endless patience they carry out their duty."*

♦

LORAN THOMPSON Where did you want us to start?

PARABOLA At the beginning! What can you tell us about obstacles? Your people have had a lot of them.

L.T. Things that get in our way?

P. Things that get in your way, that stop you; and things that although they get in your way, they don't stop you!

In the old days there were intentional obstacles: a hard life that made strong people. Then there are obstacles that come apparently from accident or human error: sometimes they are fatally destructive, and sometimes they also are strengthening to people. For instance, we are all facing the difficulties of our historical period—like this atomic waste problem, or pollution. What can we make of that? What hopes have we got?

TOM PORTER The obstacles that were put in the way of the Native American people a hundred years ago are not so different from what they are today, only now they are much more subtle. But the end result that was sought for is the same: the complete removal of the Indian nations from this land. Back in George Washington's time, and the presidents after him, it used to be the policy of the United States government to exterminate all Indians, and that was by no means a secret. It was taken by the Native people as being an official policy; whether it was or not, it was the motto of most political people at that time. They used to say: "Kill every Indian, because nits breed lice." It may not have been an official policy that was passed by Congress, but it was a state of mind at that period. So the United States government set about trying to carry that out, and there were many wars and so on, but for some reason they were not able to exterminate us. Perhaps it was because enough of the people that make up the government became outraged and had enough influence and power to stop at least the physical killing; however that happened, it did happen.

But the intention of removing all traces of the Indian people didn't stop. In place of physical violence, missionaries set out working first of all to remove all the values that make a person know what is right and what is wrong, that let a person know where he stands in the world, that let a people know where they stand in relation to other peoples of the world. The missionaries set out to remove those values and put European, Christian values in their place. It seemed to us that under the guise of education, in those days and up to today there was the same policy to attack the brains of the Native people in order to completely erase every trace of anything that gives a Native person a value system to compare what is right with what is wrong, and to instill a whole new network of thinking, completely. In sociology—is that what they call what they teach you in college?—they make graphs that show what happens when you do this to a people—take their brain out and put another in. There is a graph that shows the people going down, down, down, but when you get to a certain point, there is a name for that that I have forgotten: at that point you either shoot right straight back up to where you started, or else almost the entire race commits suicide. What is that term in sociology? Do you know what I am talking about? Well, that's the point we are at now—the Indian people. So that's why in Indian country there is such a high rate of suicide—higher in proportion to the population than any other ethnic group in this country. Many of our people are at that point now.

So those are obstacles that have been created intentionally and then after a while the intent was removed, but it was like an inherited way of doing. The intent wasn't there to do that, but people sort of inherited the policy to do away with us. So now you have a race of people that have been almost completely demoralized: a race of people that have been almost completely deprived of hope, of any sense of pride, or any hope of a continued life—or it is so messed up in the brain that it can't be comprehended. Almost. We are at that very thin line right now.

JAKE SWAMP It's important that first of all we should go back to the creation: what our purpose in life is, the obstacles that get in the way of expressing what we were given, and how it's connected with what's going on today. The Creator put us here for a purpose when He made the *Onkwehonweh* (original people). He meant that we must continue into the future, taking part in our own lives and making sure that there is a special place for our grandchildren so that they can continue life as we have. The Creator meant for us to give thanks daily. For the thousands of years we've existed, each morning when we get up we offer a thanksgiving, a prayer to the Creator for all the things He's given us—our Mother Earth, from the grasses right on up to the heavens. . .

P. Is that what the chanting was this morning?

J.S. Yes. We offer this every morning. We acknowledge all these things that the Creator gives us. We offer this thanksgiving to Him, so that He doesn't take away these powers, so that our life—everybody's life—will continue. And we always ask for peace and guidance so that we don't trip over . . . obstacles!

Today it's pretty hard to express ourselves as what we were meant to be, because years back we were disturbed by another type of life. This became dominant over our own, and there was conflict. It's pretty hard to distinguish what you're supposed to be doing and what you're not supposed to be doing; it's heartbreaking sometimes.

I feel that if we had an area of land some place where we could be left alone for at least ten years—to express ourselves—we would become so peaceful again, and we would feel that power again that our grandfathers lived with a long time ago. Our minds would become one again with nature, and we would absorb the power that nature has, because we're part of it.

L.T. Right in the beginning when He gave us all our ceremonies, and He gave us our instructions, He put it in our hands. He instructed us: "It's your responsibility to teach your children what I have given you. And it's your responsibility to make sure that it's not lost." He said, "When you come home, you make sure that you have these things with you." Because He's going to talk to us in our own language and ask our names.

So we're responsible, and that's what keeps us going. It's a big responsibility when you've got somebody's Uncle Sam over you trying to take it away from you. But we were given a prophecy; we were told what was going to happen.

P. What is the end of that prophecy?

J.S. Purification. We don't know what it means. We just have to watch out for it. They say that only a few people will be left to begin again—at a certain point. And it has happened before.

P. But it is prophesied that there will be a new birth after this destruction?

J.S. Yes. Then it starts over again.

L.T. The Hopis have a good explanation of that—the different worlds we're in. The way *we*'re told is that towards the end you'll see a really big group that believe in nothing and don't care about anything. Then you have a smaller group that's in between—that don't know which way to go. And then there's a real small group who are still holding on to what the Creator has given us and who are still trying to live by that. They're the ones that will be told where to go at a certain time in order to live through the purification.

P. For some the purification means the end; for others it means the beginning.

L.T. The end of the beginning and the beginning of the end.

P. But nothing is said about the form this purification will take?

L.T. No. Just that He's going to wash the world. That's the only way it's described.

J.S. In our opening thanksgiving we give thanks to the Thunderers for bringing water to us. But there is something else. A long time ago there were great serpents walking all over the earth; then the Creator saw that man could not live with these serpents and beasts, so He put them under the ground, and He put the Thunderers in charge to hold them there beneath the ground. If they would surface one day in the future, just to see them would destroy the people. What I understand it to mean is the uranium—it's surfacing now, they're taking it from the ground.

P. But Tom was speaking of a point where either something completely disappears, or it comes up. It seems to me there is an upsurge, the signs of a possibility at least, not only in your race but in mine, when there are people who are eager to listen to you, eager to find out what your secrets are that we have forgotten or never knew; a re-evaluation of a relationship that has gone, as you say, almost to the point of no return. Do you think there is a possibility to seize this point and come up again? How have you kept alive that very thin hope, in spite of the incredible difficulties you have had?

T.P. Well—I guess you might say that power comes from those Native people who have received the knowledge or instruction from their elders— the people who went before and who always protected this knowledge, almost in an underground way. Over the years they have had the power or the capability of forewarning, or having a knowledge of the future. That is something that can't be explained like arithmetic. It is something that is or is not; you possess it or you don't. For some reason the Native people have been very susceptible to that kind of power. In a sense, it is something like the instinct of animals. I've read that when there is an earthquake coming, even the frogs all know it; they don't have an instrument to measure how much vibration occurs under the earth, yet a simple frog—he never went to college!—has a power that even Einstein doesn't have. And this is similar to what I am talking about with the Native people, or any people who are more in tune or more open to receive such powers, or gifts—gifts, I should say. Because the Native people's philosophy of life before the arrival of European people has been one of Nature, based on Nature completely. I imagine that is why probably more Native people are extra sensitive—those who still have been somewhat

© Lee B. Ewing

protected, or managed to protect themselves against the effects of the outside world, which has a tendency to make people numb and not sensitive to anything.

So I can't talk about it like I would say one and one make two. The only thing I can say is that the philosophy of Indian life, the harmony of spiritual knowledge that we were taught by our elders, is so *simple*—perhaps that is the difficulty. It seems the people of the United States and Canada aren't satisfied unless there is a very complicated network of things to understand—then it's worthwhile! But the Indian people were too simple to let life just go unnoticed. So people ask us things now, because we do know; our grandfathers and grandmothers explained to us, when we were kids just growing up, what is going to happen and what we were going to see in our lifetimes.

They told us to stick together; they told us not to let our ways die; they told us to continue our ceremonies, and they explained the things that were going to happen. We could say that it was just a story they told us to keep us doing things the way they wanted; but they said we would see the fish turn their bellies to the sun and they would die, the fish; and now we see that, and that is why we have to listen to them, because with our own eyes we see it is true.

So that is what we have to do now with our children: tell them what is going to happen to them within ten or fifteen years. It is easier now to see—you don't have to be a psychic! It is just too evident, all over. It's evident now that people are going to destroy themselves. And it will be, because there isn't any hope that the population of the world is going to be saved, because it has gone beyond that now. But we do know that there will be certain ones of this race and certain ones of other races that will survive through these trying times when the world is going to change, who will enter into another world; but there will only be small groups of them. Most of the people are going to be done away with, because they don't want to listen or do what is right. So in that sense there is no hope, for the world population as a whole.

We know there is going to be a purification coming—pretty soon, very, very soon. A lot of times when we spoke with Canadian or American people, they said: "You are so pessimistic; why be so pessimistic?" We don't see that as pessimistic, or hopeless, but as a renewal of hope. Because the sooner the price of oil goes to ten dollars a gallon, the better for us all; the sooner the people of this world start to wake up and to get rid of the mafias that are running the country, the better for all people it will be—not just for the people, but better for everything that lives. The birds are going to be happier, the deer and the other animals will be happier, the fish will be happier, the rivers will be happier.

J.S. The most important thing for us is the freedom to express our own culture, to practice our own language. Even though most young people don't understand the language anymore, we're trying hard to bring that back—so they don't lose it. In our Freedom School, the children are taught in Mohawk. Schooling, with radio and TV, has been destroying our culture. It's not destroyed yet—it's still here in spite of everything, but not on a large scale.

P. It's destroying *our* culture too, you know. We really are all in this together!

J.S. This is what we are looking at—into the future. Today, we sit here; we watch the world around us; at the same time our forefathers gave us certain prophecies that have been ingrained in us. Our own grandfathers that we knew in our lifetime have told us in storytelling that they were told long ago that you have to watch the world as it progresses; there will be certain changes taking place that will be like markers that we're close to purification. There are a lot of processes that we're going through already—like the trees dying, and the air; they say it will be like a dark cloud coming over and it will be hard to see the sun—that's how dark it will be getting. And then the rivers will get dirty, and the fish will rise up to the top on their bellies—they will die. Some of these things have already happened.

Women are taking it upon themselves to do away with life by using birth control. That's not natural. It's against the natural order. If we look back to the past, whenever man has gone against nature it always has come back on him later.

I think the whole world needs to come to an understanding—maybe a conference could be held some place where all these things could be put on the table for everyone to look at and re-evaluate; then work from there for the future. It's the survival of mankind that we're concerned with. It's not just for ourselves. We're going through these struggles, sure, but it's our *duty* to do this. We have to do this. We have no choice. That's what our laws and our constitution tell us. *And* we have no choice but to defend ourselves. But if we perish, then I think that everyone else will too.

I think the world would listen now, at this point, because there's evidence now everywhere—you can't miss it. It's the destruction of the earth, our mother. We look at the earth like it's our own mother. It's hard to rip her up. It's a great sin for the people in the world to be doing this.

P. What is the responsibility of people who see it this way and are concerned with a rebirth?

T.P. What can be done? It is even hard to find what is practical. Everything is so unrealistic; how do you apply practicalness to it? You might say that to get some dynamite and blow up these chemical plants right away—that's the most realistic and practical thing, on the one hand; on the other hand, it isn't practical. It's confusing, because it's those very things that are destroying our kids' chance to live. It's those very things that are destroying the values to share in a peaceful life of a society of brothers to brothers, or cousins to cousins.

P. But those things are just the symptoms of something much deeper, that you can't blow up; an attitude, a way of thinking—or a way of *not* thinking, maybe.

T.P. But as long as those things have us in their grip, it's hard to consider anything else. It's the foremost thing. If you don't blow up the places that represent greed and destruction of life, then the only other thing to do is to try to make as many people as possible find the alternative to that. That's why we always support the self-sufficiency programs that young people especially are doing, in the United States and Canada and other parts of the world—with some kind of natural technology that works with the environment instead of against it.

What it really boils down to is: How valuable are the kids, the ones near you and me who are parents and grandparents? How valuable? That is the real question. Or do we just philosophize and theorize about the whole thing?

P. Do you have priests?

L.T. No, spiritual leaders—the faith keepers and the chiefs. They're just ordinary people. They're not looked on as priests or anything like that—just men and women.

P. Men *and* women? Women do ceremonies?

L.T. They bring it to the surface whenever a ceremony has to be done. They say: "The berries are ready. We ask that the ceremony take place." They name the date and the time and how it's going to be done. They ask the chiefs, and the chiefs come back and say: "Yes," and it's carried out.

P. Do you have anything that corresponds to the sacrificial dance of the Plains Indians, the Sun Dance?

J.S. Yes, in fact, some of our women left on Friday, and they went to another reservation, Six Nations, to take part in a Sun and Moon Dance. But it's a *thanksgiving* to the sun, which represents the men, and the moon, which is connected to women.

L.T. At that time, the women are told their duties and their responsibilities. And when the young men go through *their* ceremony, they're told their duties and responsibilities. It prepares them . . .

J.S. Sort of a graduation . . .

L.T. . . . for manhood.

P. You have a stronger respect for the family than is usual these days, but the children have to go to ordinary American schools, don't they?

L.T. We're trying to come up with alternatives to the school system, where we have more control over what's being taught. In the public school system we have no voice. If a teacher wants to tell the Indian students that they're pagans, that they believe in nothing, that they have nothing, that they're nothing at all—she can do that! And there'll be no one there to tell her she's wrong.

P. You're talking about wanting your own country, to practice your own ways in. It doesn't seem as if it's ever possible on any big scale for anyone to go back in time. Whether we like it or not, we're influenced, we have to go with the times. At the same time, we have to fight what's wrong with the times.
In education, for instance: you know you need certain kinds of technical education.

J.S. We realize we can't do away with all these things. We know life continues and things change. If it doesn't interfere with the way we respect the earth, then it's all right. What we're concerned with is the values of our people, the values and respect we hold for the land. This is what our survival means to us—that we have the freedom to express ourselves as we are as people. We no longer have our territory to live in as our forefathers did. It would be impossible. But we have to have a certain area where we can satisfy our own selves, our own people, about our own teachings.

P. How do you reconcile the fact that cars, airplanes are all part of the weapons of destruction, but we all use them? We don't think we can get along without them. You do too. How do you understand that?

J.S. It's probably like everything else that's going on against nature—it will have to disappear.

P. It's really hard to see the right way, isn't it? But maybe it's easier to *see* than to do.

T.P. That's my problem, and that's the first thing that comes to my mind when I see that plant over there. Because in the St. Lawrence River here—how many different kinds of poison are in there, at least that they know about? PCB's, fluoride, mercury, and all that. The Mohawk people love to eat fish; we have eaten fish for thousands of years—and for the last five hundred years, out of this river. If we go without fish for a little while we get starving for it. And those fish have those poisons in them, and we know what the scientists found out in Japan; they call that mercury poisoning from fish "Minamata disease." You can eat it now, and sometimes it won't take effect for fifteen years, but then it could hit you. But we want to eat fish so bad, and we still do; but we try to cut down—like trying to cut down on cigarettes, it's hard to quit eating fish. Our bodies want it.

That is just one thing. Now we can talk about those other two plants over there. What else comes out of them? There's a big dump right here, and when those guys from Cornwall go over there to get aluminum out, they have got holes in their shoes and in their clothes, because whatever is in the dump eats right through them. So we don't know how much of that comes through the ground into our water here. It's only a little way—you can throw a stone four times and you will be right in the middle of the dump.

Each day that goes by, our children become less and less of a human being, and our people become less and less of a people with any kind of sensitivity. Because the longer time goes by, the more our senses and our feeling of how to relate to one another as a family, whether a nuclear family or a whole-world family, become more and more numbed; and we become more and more each day living zombies.

P. There have been territories that the courts have admitted did belong to you, so there has been a reimbursement of so many million dollars. But that isn't what you really want, is it? What would you do with the money? And if you did get it, it would probably be the very worst thing you could have.

J.S. It's a destructive force, that money. Our territories are still intact. They were encroached upon. They were never sold out. But the government is going to the individual nations, trying to make them sell. That's against our constitution. In order to have any kind of dealings, you have to come as a whole united body and make that decision.

The Tribal Councils that have been placed in our territories have accepted money. But our teaching is that you can't sell our mother, and this is what the government doesn't understand. They want the title, but we can't

© Lee B. Ewing

give it. It doesn't even belong to us; it belongs to the children. We're just here to take care of it.

L.T. Like he says, the Mohawk nation's lands are still intact. Nobody has ever sold our territory, legally, and if we were to decide at this time that we need to move out of here, and we have to go somewhere where we can become stronger, then we're going to do that. Because that land out there is still ours, and it's still rightfully ours—anywhere out there in New York State. We can move into Seneca territory, Onondaga, because we're a confederacy. There's unity. But we'd like to move into our own territory. But the non-Indian people in that area wouldn't understand what we're trying to do. And right away they'd say: "That's my land because I paid for it." But they don't look back and see how they got that land. And our people wind up fighting a war. Then the way of life, the beliefs, become secondary, because you have to first protect yourselves. At this hour, we're trying to come up with different ideas that can go around armed confrontation with the state.

P. Are you getting any help here, in terms of the pollution of your land, from the various environmental groups that are fighting the government— are they incorporating your problem in their fight?

J.S. There are people studying the situation on our behalf, and most of the groups that exist have come to us. They want us to take things up with the courts, but we don't have the funds to do that. We have sent complaints to the United States government—from one nation to another nation—formal complaints.

L.T. What's happened here with the Reynolds factory problem is the Mohawk Canadian Band Council put in a suit for pollution damages, and the court ruled that the Canadian Band Council doesn't have the authority to put in the suit. They say that land that's been polluted belongs to the Queen. They also ruled that Reynolds was not sitting on New York State property. Alcoa hasn't been paying taxes because they say they're sitting on Indian lands.

P. How extraordinary! They *claim* that they're trespassing; they claim that they're illegal!

THREE MOHAWK CHIEFS • 139

L.T. And that gives us a little loophole, you see. As the people here become stronger and united, we can stand on the decision that that judge made. It will be hard, but we have the support of the different environmental organizations.

P. Are any of the people coming back to the Longhouse?

L.T. A lot of them.

J.S. There's only a handful of people who make any kind of social change—that will come right out and do things. But later on the rest of the people come out and support them. They've been learning; they've realized what they have to do: they have to defend their own nation. There was a decision by the county court against us ruling that we're not Mohawks anymore; we're the St. Regis Indians. They used some anthropologist's report as evidence.

T.P. There's quite a story to that: we used to let American people come to the Longhouse, to the ceremonies there, but we had a lot of trouble with the white people. There was this anthropologist came in there and just shoved people aside to sit down. Then he kept asking: "What did they say? What are they doing?" We told him: "Wait till after this is over, and we'll tell you." But he just kept on asking and interrupting. Another time he went to a social dance, and they told him he could come but not to tape-record anything, because these are our songs and dances. But he did; he sneaked a tape recorder in there. As a result of that the Council said that no more American people could come to our ceremonies, and they didn't permit him to come to the Longhouse anymore. And you know what he did? He threatened to bring suit against the Mohawk people for discrimination on religious grounds!

And then, you know? When the judge in Malone made that ruling against us, he used this man's work against us to make a decision.

P. No!

T.P. Yes! I'm not kidding you a bit. Instead of coming and asking us what our tradition is and what we believe, he goes by what this man says a Mohawk is. So that's how the judge said there was no more Mohawk nation.

P. What do you do about that?

J.S. Well, it doesn't really concern us what they do in the courts. We won't recognize the courts.

P. You won't try to win in the courts? You know, that *is* possible!

L.T. But if you win, you lose. Because if you're forced into the court, then you have to come under its jurisdiction.

P. Yes, you're starting to deal with a government that you say has no jurisdiction over you. You're allowing them to make a judgment on you when your position is that they don't have any right to do that, right?

J.S. That's why we have people going to Geneva, to the U.N. That's why other countries are putting in complaints against the United States on our behalf. We're being heard.

I think there's been a lot accomplished in the last few years in uniting the Mohawk people—not only the Mohawk people, but different parts of the confederacy will look over here and say: "There's something going on over there." There's some kind of unity here.

We just have to hold on as long as we can until the people out there will come together and realize that. We're waiting for them to come to realize they are Mohawk people: they are the people of the *Haudenosaunee*, and they can't go around it.

P. Everything is completely joined in your way of life: your religion, your government, your education. But some of your people have been converted to Christianity; was that a problem? Or was it very easy for them to come back to the traditional religion?

J.S. A lot of them have come back, but it's hard for them. The Christianity that was taught to them was true fear. It's pretty hard to break away from that—when you go to school and the priest tells you if you go to the Longhouse, you're going to go to Hell.

P. Is that mostly Catholic?

J.S. Yes. And this was a *priest* who stressed that to the little children growing up. So when they mature to adults they are afraid to express themselves as Mohawks, because they're afraid they'll go to Hell, I guess!

P. They're never taught to make friends with the devil?

J.S. No!

P. But you know, that's just "churches," that's not *religion*.

L.T. That's right.

P. True religions aren't *against* each other. They couldn't be. *Churches* are, though, and that's where the trouble comes in, and now most religions have become churches.

Didn't you have some Buddhist monks living with you here, when you had your encampment?

L.T. Yes—in some tents by the river.

P. What do you call your own government?

J.S. The Council of Chiefs or the Longhouse Council mostly.

P. Can you tell us how the chiefs are chosen?

J.S. By the Clan Mothers.

L.T. Very carefully!

P. When they grow up or when they're little? Are they trained to be chiefs? This is a part of the woman's role that interests us.

J.S. As for the women's role: they're the ones that have the children. The women know the children best—they know their faults and their dislikes. They watch the children grow up so they know who's suited for any kind of position.

P. But then do they all together come to an agreement? Is there one woman in particular who . . .

J.S. The woman who takes care of that—from that one long extended family—the title's thousands of years old—the one who happens to be "standing," she's the one that picks the chief.

L.T. The Clan Mother is chosen by all the people to take care of the position of the chiefs, to make sure that the chiefs are "standing," or carrying out their function. And if a chief is to die, within a few days the

Clan Mother has to have picked another candidate for that position. She has to go through her own clan to do that. The Clan Mother would call her clan together to notify them of the person she chooses for this position.

There are three Clan Mothers and three chiefs in each of the three clans—Wolf, Turtle, and Bear—nine chiefs, nine Clan Mothers. So the Clan Mother of the chief who died would call the whole clan together and choose someone from her own clan.

P. Can she choose from another clan?

J.S. No, not unless they run out of people who can fulfill the position in her own clan. Then they have to borrow from another clan. It doesn't happen too often.

L.T. And if she doesn't do her job properly, then the clan can replace her too.

J.S. And she has the power to replace the chief if he doesn't do this duty. She'll take him outside the Council and scold him. He has three chances. At the third warning—she takes his horns, his title, away, and she'll pick another one.

P. It's an extraordinary system—and it works too, doesn't it?

L.T. It works.

It has to go through the clan first. When the candidate is brought into the open, then she says: "Is there anyone here that has anything against this person—who doesn't want him to hold this position for the clan?" Then, if there's no one at that time, he goes on to the meeting of the whole Longhouse. That same question is put up in front of the people. If anyone has a valid question or has any doubts in their mind about that person, it's brought out at that time. If not, it's mentioned in the ceremony that if objections haven't been brought out before, then it's never to be brought out in the future.

P. It's like the banns in the Christian marriage ceremony: if there's no objection now, "forever after hold thy peace"!

And you have special war chiefs?

L.T. They're chosen at different times. It's like a temporary position.

THREE MOHAWK CHIEFS • 143

Whenever there's a problem, there always seems to be one or two people that stand out and lead naturally. Many times, they're the ones that are chosen to hold that position. But then when the problem is over, their job is finished and they just guide and watch over the men so that they're organized.

P. How do you know when a problem is over? Because sometimes it changes into another one . . . speaking of obstacles. . .

L.T. Well, then, it's just the start of another problem. We're used to that!

A lot of what you said a little while ago—that it's not realistic to think that we can go back and live the way they lived so many years ago . . . a lot of people throw that at us. They're saying: "They want to go back and live like we lived a hundred and fifty years ago; run around in the woods. . . ." That's not what we want. We just want to be able to live in peace amongst ourselves, amongst the non-Indians, and be able to carry out our own functions, carry out our own ceremonies, our own governmental administration, and be left alone. But we want to be respected by people coming into our territory—just like we respect other ways when *we* go to Ottawa, Toronto, Washington, whatever. We don't go against the grain. But when they come into our area, they want to bring in their own laws and force them on us.

P. Yes, but there's a certain problem there. In the piece you wrote for the *Akwesasne Notes*, Jake, you had a wonderful analogy: you were in your canoe and the Dutch were in their boat, and you couldn't put a foot in both, or you'd fall in the river and drown. Right? The two boats could go along the river side by side, but people could not cross from one to the other.

So: is this possible? You want to be left alone; you also want some of the things that would be an exchange with white people.

L.T. That comes in another prophecy, when we are told that certain things were going to happen. First we were given the ceremonies. We went on for quite a few hundred years just living by the ceremonies. Then we were told when we were given the Great Law of Peace: "You're going to see a light-complected, blue-eyed person coming to your shores, and along with him, he's going to have certain articles that you have to leave alone, because it's going to make you go astray and take you away from what I've given you." Then for quite a few years we lived according to the Great Law of Peace, and then came these articles—religion, and money, gambling—things like that—which take you right away from the Creator. It came about that a lot of our people were using all these things, and then we were given another message: "Now you people have accepted a lot of these things, so now we have to give you another message. There are certain things that you can use: you can use the house, but it's a home; it's just a shelter. Don't make a house that's going to make another person who can't build a house like that jealous. Keep it in mind that way—don't flaunt it."

You take other things like that—TV is a bad thing, the way it's used today, but you can use it like we're using it now: we're bringing the people back together, to try to get the truth out to the people. As long as you use it properly and don't use it just to destroy, it's there to use.

P. But we have to accept the bad with the good. Television and radio are good for some things, and cars and modern medicine and modern education—and they're bad for other things. If you accept those things, it seems to me that you accept that there are drawbacks. There are obstacles.

J.S. The only thing I can say to that is that we have to continue—do the best we can according to our teachings. If we see that something's going to be destructive—like trucks carrying nuclear waste across our bridges—then we have to speak out against it. We can't just hide and take it. Our people have a natural instinct for survival.

P. You can toss things back and forth between the boats. But don't fall in!

J.S. Don't lose the balance there. People have to have respect for one another, and if they have something to offer you that they think might be good for you, then they can offer—but not force you. That's the kind of respect we want. We want to determine our own future—not to have somebody else determine it for us.

L.T. In order to give what Indian people have to the world, we have to preserve it. And we find it difficult to preserve it here because politics and government are interfering. To our minds, we have to go somewhere else where we can teach our children everything that we know—so that it gets stronger and stronger; so that more people know it. It's like at a standstill: one person dies and only one other is picking it up, so it stays in one place. And we want it to grow.

P. You're absolutely right—there are different times and stages. . . . Was it Ramakrishna who said that when a tree is small you build a fence around it so that the cows will not knock it over, but when it is grown the cows can come and sleep under its shade? That's a wonderful image, don't you think? Maybe we're at the point where you have to build a fence.

But you don't want *us* to build a fence!

L.T. It's hard for us to understand how the United States government can operate morally—without having a spiritual mind when you make a law, what do you have? Just control—control over smaller people that are trying to mind their own business.

P. I think that that's the basic thing that's wrong with the modern world: two things that absolutely have to be together have split. The spiritual life has removed itself from daily, practical life. And this is just the road to death! I don't think that will come back, except in the way that your prophecy says; I think the world *has* to be purified. Maybe there will be human seeds that will come back in a new way.

When people stop believing in something bigger than they are is when this split occurs and everything begins to go a little bit crazy. And that is why I suppose some of us turn to all the different ways in which human beings have made contact with a force higher than themselves. That is why the traditions that are still alive have something to do for us. Something has to stay alive in order to be born again.

L.T. But prophesies are given just as a warning and it's our responsibility to try to follow whatever warnings that were given—try to stop destruction from happening. That's the position of my people.

T.P. It is a hard thing. People have to do something, for sure; but what are they going to do? That's the big question. Most people in this country say they are Christians, I think; it's supposed to be a Christian country. And the Christian philosophy, just like the Indian one, has an answer to it—I think; of course, I don't know the Christian way too much, but I am impressed sometimes when I hear the preachers talking on the radio on Sundays. The man they call Jesus Christ was a man who believed in sharing everything—I think that is what they said. And when they were collecting money in the church, Jesus went in there and he was mad! He didn't say: "Please, may I talk?" He just waved his fist and started jumping around, saying: "What the hell is wrong with you people?"—or something like that. He said: "Stop the gold and silver collection!" I like that; that's true. That ought to be done. Then I heard about another time when they were having some kind of feast, and they cut the bread up so everyone would have a piece. I think even there wasn't enough bread, but a miracle was performed and there was enough so everyone could eat. They shared the bread and something else—fish. So to me, that raised the question right there: What does the United States want? What does Mr. Reagan want? What does each senator want?—And I will put the same question to Gorbachev too, and to anyone else who follows a destructive life form. I am not a pro-American; I am not a pro-Communist—I am neither; I am just a pro-human being. So if they are looking to the Christian religion, I think maybe there might be an answer there for the American people, because there too it tells about the same understanding that the Indian people have, and that is to share, and be interdependent on each other. If we can't do that then it's no use. When you talk about sharing, you get labeled a Communist. But I really think everyone has got to share; there can't be rich and poor people; there's got to be just brothers. But that is too simple—too simple.

All our ceremonies are founded on Nature. There's the Midwinter ceremony; the Maple Leaf ceremony; the Planting ceremony; the Mother Earth ceremony; the Thunder and the Sun and the Moon ceremonies; the Wind ceremony; the Corn and the Bean and the Strawberry ceremonies. That is what our life is about, our whole religious understanding is about everything in the world that helps us to live. We are dependent on those things. So we are a very practical people in our beliefs; we base them on the practical things in the world we live in. Maybe that is where we are a little bit different, because I notice the preachers when they talk on the radio on Sunday, they talk about hoping for the Good Land and entering the pearly gates of heaven. I think they made a little mistake, because you must try here first before you worry about over there; now is the time to worry, to do something now. Our religion doesn't worry about the after-life, but about what we do today.

P. You worry about your children's life—not your after-life, but how they can survive.

T.P. Yes—at least that *the bed will be made*. Because my mother and my grandmother made the bed for me so that I could have a comfortable sleep. This world is a bed. And so our duty is to do the same thing our grandmothers did. There are seven generations ahead that we have the responsibility for; so we have to watch out not to do anything to hurt them.

I don't know how to convince the American or Canadian people or any others that need to be convinced of that. You hear them say: "I worked hard for what I have, and when my children grow up they have to do the same thing. I've done my share." So many Americans say that, it's pitiful. So then when the parents get old, that's why the younger people don't care if they throw them into an old-age home, because they didn't care about them when they were growing up—not really.

P. That's a serious problem, because the family seems to have disintegrated in Western society.

T.P. It looks like it. Here, our grandmothers and grandmothers and grandfathers and grandfathers—you see, we don't have just two of each, every old person we call grandmother or grandfather—

P. But the young people call each other grandmother and grandfather, too; Loran said Jake was his grandfather, and then they both said you were their grandfather!

T.P. That's a joke!
So that's one big difference I see in the two mentalities. It's a very good thing to have many grandparents because you honor someone when you call them that. Here, we know even our tenth cousins; because we all live within fourteen miles, and we see each other every day. In America, grandparents are in one place and the grandchildren are all over the world. There's no real family; the day-to-day relationship of grandparents isn't there. The family is very important. We were talking about education; that's the biggest thing in the breakdown of the family, Western education,

because it takes the children away from their mother and father. A complete stranger teaches them. That's why there's no heart anymore in family life.

There are so many ways that have to be tried, and a lot of them fail; and the thing is, there isn't so much time to try things anymore. People have got to become more serious about that.

P. Loran was saying before we sat down together that even though the whole concept of a reservation was to put you down, in the end it turns out to be something that gives you strength, because you are all together, at least. Though it was an attempt to cast you aside, it's been something that has kept you together.

T.P. Yes—that's for sure. That's true. In fact, you know, here among the Akwesasne Mohawk people, the European people divided us so much by the rules of "divide and conquer" that came from England; they planted many of the seeds of division here. And we haven't been together for so long, because some of our people have become Catholic and some Methodists and Mormons, and there are those who remain traditional. But there is still something here among the people in this particular community, so that no matter how many generations went through the process of assimilation, there were some powerful means of the Creator that have not permitted the most sophisticated methods of divide and conquer to penetrate completely. There is something here that is undefinable in this community, Akwesasne: I don't know if it's Mohawk, Indian, or what it is, but perhaps when I said that we live within fourteen miles and know our tenth and fifteenth cousins, so we are all one big, big, big family numbering about seven thousand, maybe that is it. So all that New York State has put us through has caused the Mohawk people to recognize a common enemy. And that has united us. We have been separated for years. But now we are coming together. So the United States in its attempt to do away with my people have caused them to unite. They have done us a service; sure.

I don't see that we are pessimistic in our outlook; because if the world started to shake in this next hour, and the dam broke over there, so what if the water took us as it came through and drowned us as we sit here? We would say: "It wiped it out and cleaned it up good! We must have been part of the problem!"

And then laugh about it too—yes! Because we deserved it, if that happened to us. But if we are right—only the Mystery of this world would know that, and decide if we are going to the next world or not, or if we are going to be weeded out like the weeds in the garden. So that is not being pessimistic: because I am only as good as you and you and the others here; I am only as good as the fish in that river; I am only as good as the grass in this field. Because if that is destroyed, I will be destroyed with it. I can't do anything if the river breaks the dam; I can't stop it, no matter how much I yell. It is out of my hands. That isn't pessimistic; that is just the facts.

11

◆

An Interview with
Tara Tulku, Rinpoche

"Pilgrimage," VOL. IX:3, August, 1984

A New Dwelling

By the standards of his own rigorous tradition, the Venerable Tara Tulku, Rinpoche, is a remarkable individual. Born in Khams, eastern Tibet, in 1927, Rinpoche was recognized at a very early age as the reincarnation of the previous abbot of neighboring Sendru Monastery. Beginning his monastic training at Sendru at the age of three, Rinpoche in 1940 entered Drepung Monastery, the largest in Tibet, with ten thousand monks. There he was recognized as master of all five fields of Buddhist scholarship at the age of twenty-nine—inordinately young for such an achievement. He proceeded for advanced training to Gyuoto Tantric Monastery, where he remained until the Chinese invasion—making him one of the last monks to receive a complete Tibetan Buddhist training on his native soil.

The great catastrophe of 1959 decimated Gyuoto Tantric Monastery; of five hundred monks in residence, only seventy escaped. After great hardships, the monastery was relocated in India, where Tara Tulku guided it through the arduous process of reconstruction. Following nine years as abbot—three times the customary tenure—Rinpoche became abbot emeritus. But his work continues unabated. His Holiness the Dalai Lama has appointed him to teach the Dharma to Westerners each year at the Tibetan monastery at Bodhgaya, and he has taught in America both as the Henry R. Luce Professor of Comparative Religious Ethics at Amherst College in Amherst, Massachusetts, and as scholar-in-residence at the American Institute for Buddhist Studies in Amherst.

We spoke to Tara Tulku at the home of Robert A.F. Thurman, Professor of

Religion at Amherst College, a founder of the American Institute of Buddhist Studies, and the man who was instrumental in bringing Tara Tulku to the United States. Professor Thurman not only translated for us with vigor and wit, but helped illuminate difficult aspects of Tibetan teaching during the course of our long conversation. His translating skills came into play as soon as Rinpoche joined us, smiling brightly, arms spread wide in greeting, dressed in a monastic garb of maroon robes, yellow silk shirt, and red sweater bearing a portrait pin of H.H. the Dalai Lama.

After lunch, we gathered in Tara Tulku's sunny upstairs living quarters where he sat on Western-style pillows. As he responded to our questions with warmth and intensity, we were aware of his openness and freedom and of our own instinctive respect toward him. His fluid attention, sense of humor, great intellectual depth, and—it seemed to us—profundity of being gave his responses, and his silences, a rare seriousness and weight.

♦

PARABOLA Rinpoche, perhaps we could start out by asking what connotations pilgrimage has for you.

TARA TULKU We believe that there are two reasons to go on pilgrimage. One is temporary, the other is ultimate. Generally, we feel that pilgrimage is very important and powerful. If we were to go on pilgrimage in the way it is recommended in the Buddha Dharma, it would be truly excellent for us. For example, the places where we live, our dwellings, are not quite right or suitable. Why is that? Because no matter how we deal with them, they become a source of suffering for us. Similarly, our ordinary body is definitely not proper as it is. Therefore, it is necessary that we contemplate the development and acquisition of a new dwelling, a new body. You can say that the Buddha Dharma, its various techniques and arts, consists of means for developing and attaining a new body, a new dwelling. There are both ordinary and extraordinary methods for creating these; the process of going on pilgrimage should be understood as part of these methods.

P. Is Rinpoche referring to the development of a subtle body in this lifetime?

T.T. We will come around to the subject of subtle bodies and such, but we haven't quite gotten there yet! Let's consider the case of Śakyamuni Buddha, to commemorate whom one goes on the pilgrimage to Bodhgaya. On the ordinary level of reality, Śakyamuni, in the series of events relating to his eating the first bit of rice, taking his bath, going to the Bodhi tree and so forth, realized a new body. He suddenly became golden, and his ascetic body filled out. He had a completely different body—it suddenly appeared on the ordinary level.

The place itself, under the Bodhi tree at Bodhgaya, was transformed as well. It became a place of diamond, a *vajra* place, a place of extreme sacredness. Why is it sacred? Because Buddha's transformative experience of unexcelled perfect enlightenment blessed it in a special way. Some people even believe that if you reach and stand on that place and take the Bodhisattva vow or make prayers to achieve Buddhahood for the benefit of all beings, then just because of the power of that place, you will never be reborn in the lower states. And if you meditate there, recite prayers, and study, the place has a special power for the mind to come to realization. It is a place of light and bliss. This is because this is the place where Śakyamuni achieved the special Buddha body, a body which has only bliss and happiness, and never suffers. He also used this place as a basis for perceiving all places as indivisible from the highest heaven of the four realms. Because this place was the basis from which he re-envisioned all reality as the highest heaven, it is extremely sacred.

That's how Buddhists explain this. But when we hear it, we have to ask ourselves whether it could really be so. There is, however, an excellent example that it really is so which the Buddhists use. We say, when we go to a battlefield, that it is a horrible, awful place. And if we go to such a place, we become uncomfortable and sad.

P. Are there actually physical forces at work in such places, or is this a result of memories connected with these places?

T.T. Both. Bodhgaya has a great special power infused in it by a person whose achievement was timeless, in the sense that the future was present. It lasts. Also, if one goes there with a strong vision of that moment, as if it were not separated from one, as if it were not past, then the power is much greater. But even when someone not thinking of its importance wanders through Bodhgaya, it has a very great power. Many people have remarked upon this.

P. Just as there are places that can be beneficial and places that can be detrimental, it can be said that there are paths that lead towards a true goal, and paths that lead towards falsehood. How can one discern whether one is on a right path—particularly if one lives outside of a traditional society?

T.T. The impact on the mind is how one judges the validity of the path. Here, again, the issue of relativity is crucial. When a path brings us into relativities, into causes and conditions that influence the mind in a positive way, we can say that the path is positive or good. But how have you asked this question?

P. We are thinking of pilgrimage as not just a physical voyage, but as the journey from ignorance to enlightenment.

T.T. Yes, you are jumping ahead of me again! I am talking first about the ordinary level of pilgrimage. For example, we have Bodhgaya, a place to which anyone can go, but an especially sacred place. And if one has faith in the Buddha, and practices and meditates and proceeds on the path from ignorance to enlightenment, the place gets a greater and greater power for one. Now, this is what we mean by ordinary pilgrimage.

As for extraordinary pilgrimage, we believe that there is a place, made by the Buddha's merits, realizations, and vows and prayers for all sentient beings, which exists on a subtle level. He has created this place from his achievement of the timelessness in which past, present, and future are equally accessible. In this place, he receives those beings who go there. But this place is practically impossible for us to encounter from our ordinary level.

The Buddha left there an inconceivable body, an extraordinary one which has not passed away as the ordinary one has. These are the two major foci of pilgrimage on the extraordinary level. Why is that? Because the Buddha has said that if one reaches ethical, meditational, and intellectual achievement of a certain kind, then one can come to have such a dwelling, such a body and mind. One becomes a Buddha oneself. If one practices according to those teachings, one can transform one's world, one's body, and one's mind. That is the true inner pilgrimage—the attainment of enlightenment; to change the body and the world as well as the mind.

P. What is the connection or meeting point between ordinary and extraordinary pilgrimage?

T.T. You can see ordinary pilgrimage as a kind of preparation, as the creation of a paradigm in the mind, and as an accumulation of merit for the person who will then go on the extraordinary pilgrimage when he becomes capable of it. The nearer one gets to the field of those activities of the Buddha, the historical and transhistorical realities of those activities, the more one generates faith, admiration, and estimation of his achievements, and the more one prizes one's achievement of these stages oneself. The more one likes something, the more likely it is that in the future one will acquire it.

One thing that isn't well enough known is that the Buddha himself, in his own discourses, gave the recommendation to undertake ordinary pilgrimage. It's not something that others added after his death. In the Parinirvana Sutra, when the Buddha is about to die, he says to Ananda that Buddhas always die in this way, and that after they die, the relics are put in a stupa, much bigger than for a king. Afterwards, there are four places where pilgrims should go: where a Buddha is born, where a Buddha attains enlightenment, where a Buddha first turns the Wheel of Dharma, and where a Buddha attains Parinirvana. Thus you recapitulate the whole life cycle of the Buddha by going around these four places. The Buddha seems to have been the first person to create such a pattern—that is, pilgrimage that is not just a journey to a local, ancestral, or tribal shrine.

P. Does this establish a physical relationship to the Buddha?

T.T. Exactly right.

P. Has pilgrimage, then, played a large role in the life of Tibetans?

T.T. Oh, yes. It has entered the ears of Tibetans that it is a great and sacred thing to go on pilgrimage. Some know what they are doing, and the context in which they do it, and the attitude which they should bring to it. Others go without knowing. At Bodhgaya, they take bits of earth and put them into amulets or charm boxes to take with them. This is a

Tibetan custom.

P. Does the arduousness of the pilgrimage add to the merit?

T.T. Yes. The more suffering that is undergone—provided that suffering is borne in the positive sense—the more merit accrues. Of course, if you get mad and irritated with your hardships, that will decrease the merit.

P. Has pilgrimage played an important role in your own life, Rinpoche?

T.T. Yes, it has had a great impact on my life, particularly in terms of my experiences at Bodhgaya. They have been very powerful—praying, meditating, performing ceremonies. The tremendously peaceful atmosphere at Bodhgaya has had a great effect on me. It facilitates achieving my own sense of peacefulness.

P. It's a common practice among educated Westerners to go around the world, visiting pilgrimage sites in traditions that are not their own. What do you think of, for instance, a Christian going to a Buddhist site?

T.T. It doesn't matter what religion people hold, if they are going with an open mind, if they are seeking truth. In this case, it is extremely meritorious to go to the holy sites of any religion.

P. But isn't it necessary to have a thorough training in the tradition of a site in order to fully receive the influences connected to it?

T.T. Yes, there is a question of degree of merit, but there is always some real merit. There's a famous story about a monk who was not going to be admitted to an order by some of the order's venerable elders because he was a nasty person with a bad record. The monk complained bitterly about this, saying, "You bunch of incompetent venerables, I want to be a monk! So what if I've been mean." He scolded them, in his typically abusive way, about how they shouldn't stand in his way, and how at least they should ask the Buddha before making a final decision. So the elders went and asked the Buddha, "Does this fellow have any redeeming characteristics, so that he might benefit himself and others by becoming a monk in our order?" The Buddha looked at the monk for a long time and then said, "Yes, indeed, he does have a redeeming feature." When the elders asked, "What is it?" the Buddha told this story: Many previous lifetimes ago, he said, this monk had been an ant. As an ant, he had been present when some pilgrims had held a picnic in Bodhgaya, near the stupa of the former Buddha. The ant had been sneaking around, trying to steal crumbs from the food of the pilgrims. Suddenly, one of the picnickers got up and started to circumambulate the stupa—with the ant stuck on his foot, hanging on for dear life! He held on for several revolutions around the stupa. And by virtue of that, the Buddha concluded, he was now deserving of becoming a monk in the order.

P. Could Rinpoche indicate to us what qualities a person needs to set out on the inner or extraordinary pilgrimage?

T.T. A person must have faith in the goal—faith that there is a transformed place; that there is the possibility of an evolutionary transformation of the self, of body and mind; faith that beings have done so; and that they left accurate records of how to do so. Next, effort is required. The more faith one has, and the more ambition one has in consequence of that faith, the more one's efforts will increase. And in order to generate that faith more powerfully, one must have the memory, the mindfulness, of the excellence of the goal. The more one can remember what a Buddha is, the more one's aspiration for that becomes, and the more one's effort increases. The more one realizes how beneficial that achievement is, what great advantages there are in achieving such a stage, the more intensely one will wish to practice the methods leading to such a stage. Similarly, if one is aware of a really delicious meal in a particular restaurant or country, one's effort will be more intense to go to that place to have that feast.

P. But we don't know this end state—the end of the pilgrimage—as clearly as we know the taste of food. It's something unknown by definition.

T.T. How is it that we get to know it? By depending upon the greatest of Buddha's accomplishments—his speech. A remarkable aspect of the Buddha is that he taught and described extensively the nature of all the various stages and paths. It is by relying on these descriptions that we can come to understand it.

Two aspects of the Buddha's teaching are particularly important in this context. One is that he always spoke reasonably, providing clear reasons of why it is one must come to this or that understanding. You might call this

his scientific side. And the other is his artistic side. He also spoke poetically and vividly. In his discourses, there are very vivid descriptions—evocations, you might say—of various kinds of states, of beings, heavenly realms, and so forth. So by the imagination and by critical wisdom, he has methods for both sides of the person to develop simultaneously. The initial key, of course, is to be aware that ordinary reality is the reality of suffering. And second, that suffering has a root which can be eradicated. Once that has been realized, the prospect of a state without suffering becomes tangible.

P. But what is it that distinguished someone who comes to this understanding from someone who does not? What is the nature of that critical moment that leads one to place one's foot upon the path?

T.T. As we define it, the first step in the path is the taking of refuge. Then comes the mind of renunciation and detachment, the spirit of love and compassion. Third is the wisdom of selflessness. These are the three things that are necessary.

P. And what is it that leads one person to seek refuge and another to ignore it?

T.T. This has to do with whether the two major causes of the taking of refuge are present in the person. These causes are said to be terror and faith. By faith, we mean faith in the three jewels of Buddha, Dharma, and Sangha—that there is a community, a teaching, and an enlightened being. By terror, we mean terror of cosmic suffering, especially, at the beginning, terror of the lower states of existence—of hell, of the *preta* realm, of animal suffering, terror of uncontrolled future lives. A person who has those two causes—cosmic terror of an unsaved destiny, and faith that there are compassionate beings who have the ability to give one the method of saving oneself from that terror—will automatically take refuge. That is the beginning of the path.

P. Once one is on the path, we are told that one will meet many obstacles. What is a fruitful attitude to take towards those obstacles— particularly if they seem to be other people?

T.T. We mustn't be angry with the obstacles. When obstacles arise, the key thing is to practice tolerance, one of the most transcendent virtues taught in Buddhism. One must cultivate one's patience and tolerance. Of course, there are levels wherein, in addition to not being angry with obstacles, as far as that has to do with one's subjective attitude, there are ways of going around them. There are even methods, in the tantras for example, of removing obstacles.

P. Is there a way of transforming an obstacle, or must it always be removed or gone around?

T.T. Śantideva's book, *Bodhicaryāvatāra* (*A Guide to the Bodhisattva's Way of Compassion*) is full of this sort of approach, about how your enemy is your greatest teacher—ways of turning things around. There is a very elaborate discussion in Śantideva about tolerance as a great virtue. From tolerance arises beauty. All of Buddha's beauty arises from his practice of tolerance. The more patient you become, the more you will be able to bear suffering, the more beautiful you will become. To be tolerant, however, I need an enemy. I need someone to bother me, so I can practice my tolerance. Thus the enemy becomes a guru. Śantideva is full of techniques of this kind, in a very sophisticated, intricate, beautiful form.

P. So the greatest obstacle on the path is having no obstacles at all.

T.T. Śantideva will go to such extremes as making statements like that. But on the other hand, when tolerance is perfected and one has Buddhahood, even if there are not obstacles in oneself, other beings have quite enough obstacles to go around, to provide an outlet for your tolerance. For example, the Dalai Lama is always saying that the Communists have been very kind to him, a tremendous help. But, on the other hand, he says that the Communists' destruction of his people is bad. When a soldier has beaten up an old man, or killed a monk or a child, that is bad. If you know the practice of tolerance, then an enemy can help you. But otherwise, you are simply harmed by your enemy, and experience even more harm from your own anger and bitterness at the enemy, so it's doubly bad. Nobody benefits from that. So without being angry at anyone, certainly you should try very forcefully to stop bad persons from doing bad things.

P. Is meditation in any way like a pilgrimage?

T.T. There are many ways of meditating. If one is just concentrating on a single object, then it is hard to see it as a pilgrimage. Within, however, the discursive or thematic or analytic types of meditation, some can be said to be like a pilgrimage. Again, within that, there are ordinary and extraordinary levels.

P. Even in very simple relaxation meditation, however, one encounters obstacles. One is going to a slightly freer place than the usual subjective state. It's a kind of inward journey, even on a very simple level.

T.T. Yes. We talk about these things in the form of remedies. For example, if one's mind is full of anxiety, then one contemplates the counting of breath. If one is excessively attached to something, the contemplation of unloveliness is considered to be a remedy. If one has anger, then tolerance is meditated on. Each mental imbalance has its particular corrective remedy.

P. To what extent is one's pilgrimage individual and solitary, and to what extent does it involve companions? If it is a group effort, what should one's attitude be towards one's companions on the pilgrimage?

T.T. There are various levels of pilgrimage, relating to the motivation involved. In an objective way, of course, there is always an individual and a collective component relating to any action. But the action changes and has a different degree of merit and power depending on the orientation of the person. For example, if a person is what is called an "inferior" person— that is, a spiritual, but "inferior" spiritual person—he is going on the pilgrimage to get merit for himself, to prevent his future sufferings and to achieve heavenly and other kinds of reincarnations in his future lives. This is somewhat narrow, but it has a certain type of merit. The middle person is going on a pilgrimage to get merit not only for the betterment of his life, but to achieve liberation and enlightenment for himself. This has a wider power. Finally, bodhisattvas go on the pilgrimage for themselves, but simultaneously wish all beings to go with them. In a sense, they visualize that they are taking all beings with them on that pilgrimage. They are including all beings as receiving the fruit of what they do. That becomes a vast root of virtue. These are the famous three types of person— inferior, mediocre, and superior—on the basis of how they are motivated in any virtuous action that they might do. If one goes on the pilgrimage just to benefit oneself in this life, it is not considered a religious action, but just an ordinary action, and yet one can receive some benefit from it.

P. Like the ant on the shoe!

T.T. Yes.

P. What aspects of Buddhism are most misunderstood by Westerners?

T.T. There's a long list. The worst is the misunderstanding of emptiness as if it were nothingness, leading to meditation on nothingness: non-thought. Relating to this, the notion that there's no ethics in Buddhism. And then, the wish and insistence on immediate practice of tantra.

P. Is it difficult for Tibetans to understand Buddhism?

T.T. Yes, it's very hard for anyone. It entails a whole process of education.

P. I know I have no understanding of emptiness.

T.T. You must make efforts in the method of coming to understand it. Emptiness is the essence of the Dharma.

P. Does this have something to do with it: We have a consciousness which persists; thoughts come and go, but consciousness persists. Now, there's one consciousness which is involved in, identified with, and reacting to an external reality. Is the same consciousness, when it is freed from that identification, part of what is meant by emptiness?

T.T. To think about emptiness, one has to examine how, in your mind, when you let it settle a little bit, there arises this sense of "I." You have to observe that "I" and come to understand it. That's in the direction of emptiness—not just some peacefulness. The critical insight about what that "I" is. The mind of "I," "I," "I" is always, continually arising. There is a relative "I"—the conventional self really is there. But we don't under-stand it as a relative and conventional "I," because we have a strange way of exaggerating it, and perceiving it to be an independent thing, not part of the relativity which is emptiness. The important thing is to avoid thinking of emptiness as nothingness, which comes from thinking of it as a kind of empty space of peaceful meditation. The real meaning of emptiness is relativity, relationality, interdependency.

P. So seeing this "I" come up again and again is very important.

T.T. Its purpose is to organize your activities—for example, to take the pictures you are taking, to walk, to eat, to think, to achieve Buddhahood. To help other beings. Buddha has to have an "I," an ego. You need the relative ego, you need to make it stronger, but to make it less absolute. This lets it grow more.

P. The relative ego must assume its proper place.

T.T. It's very interesting. You never lose the ego, although temporarily, because the relative ego and the hypothetical absolute ego are so inextricably intermixed, when you begin with critical wisdom to look into the absolute ego, you see through it, you see that it is just a presumption. And it seems to take the relative one with it as it disappears. You feel as if you've lost your ego. But that's an illusion. If you have a nihilistic outlook, you identify that loss of the relative "I" as a big achievement, and so you become a nihilist by experience as well—and then you are very difficult to deal with.

P. Is there any way in which the dissemination of the Dharma to the West can be seen as a kind of pilgrimage?

T.T. Since America is a new area for Buddhism, it is hard to see how one can conceive of it as a pilgrimage in the conventional Buddhist sense. However, in an unconventional sense, in the context that the metaphor of the Buddha's teaching is the Turning of the Wheel of the Dharma, and there definitely is a progression of the Dharma around the planet—it does seem that in Asia it has had a time of decline, although it is still very much there, while it is growing in the West—it can be seen as a pilgrimage. The expression for pilgrimage in Tibetan is "to turn around the place," to circumambulate a place, and we can see that the Dharma itself is circling around the globe. The whole globe is becoming a Wheel of Dharma.

12

◆

A Conversation with
Joseph Epes Brown

"The Trickster," VOL. 4:1, February, 1979

The Wisdom of
the Contrary

Joseph Epes Brown, well-known authority on Plains Indians
cultures, first came in contact with the Native American view of the world and of
nature in his boyhood, among the Northeastern and Southwestern Indians. It was
an influence that has shaped his whole life. After graduating from Haverford
College he traveled among the Plains Indians and studied Indian lore, and became
convinced that among the tribes a great and ancient wisdom was still preserved. He
was especially attracted by what he had read and heard of Black Elk, the great
Sioux medicine man, then in the last years of his long life; he determined to meet
and speak with him before he died. Following the tribe to where they were camped,
he was directed to Black Elk's lodge and stood outside for a moment in some
trepidation, not at all sure of his reception. When he entered, however, the old
shaman raised his nearly sightless eyes and said, "There you are. Why did you
take so long to come?"

Brown spent eight months with Black Elk, taking down what the old priest had
been, it seemed, waiting to tell him about the rites and ceremonies of his people.
The result was the wonderful book The Sacred Pipe, "Black Elk's book," as
Joseph Brown calls it, claiming no other title to it than that of "recorder and editor."

Brown is now teaching Native American religions at the University of Montana
at Missoula. He has built an octagonal wooden house—very much the shape of a
tepee—at the foot of St. Mary's Peak in the Bitterroot Mountains, where he lives
with his Swiss dancer wife and their four children, a number of horses which he
trains, rides, and shows, several dogs, and a varying number of buffalo. Besides

167

teaching, ranching, and writing, he travels a good deal: he is in much demand as a lecturer, he makes frequent trips to Europe, and goes often to visit his friends among the Plains tribes, hear their stories, and take part in their ceremonies.

◆

PARABOLA We want to talk to you about the clown and the trickster who play such a prominent role in Native American cultures. In our culture we tend to think of him as being there for our entertainment: the circus or rodeo clown; something to amuse the children. But perhaps even they have another, more hidden function. The rodeo clown, for instance: he isn't there simply to amuse the crowd with vulgar jokes; he's an extraordinarily brave man whose daring performances protect the riders from being trampled on if they are thrown. But how could they be related, for example, to the Contraries of the Plains people?

JOSEPH EPES BROWN Before we get into details such as Contraries and the Plains people's traditions, would it be possible to talk a little bit about the meaning of the general phenomenon of "clowns" across cultures, and then come to specific references to American Indian cultures? I have some very strong feelings about this that I would like to verbalize, if I can.

I would like to emphasize first that we are here talking about "clowns," Contraries, or Trickster beings within essentially religious contexts—that is to say, within traditional societies. When we talk about clowns in our society, such as the rodeo clown or the Barnum and Bailey circus clown, we are dealing with a different perspective, because here clowns and clowning occur outside a traditional religious context, although perhaps this is not so true in the origins of the circus. But today one could say that in our society—and this is perhaps not a kindly remark—clowns don't have the quality of impact they do in traditional societies because it seems that in a society such as ours, everybody tends to be some kind of a clown, and life so often has the mood of a carnival, that the sacred context within which the traditional clown acts has become lost.

P. Yes, it's not very kind, but perhaps that's true.

J.B. Because with us, the carnival or the acts of a clown amuse but do not lead towards religious understanding or spiritual realization. In traditional societies in general, however, I would say that the role of the clown serves an enormously important purpose in that it opens a door, in a very subtle and effective way, into a realm of greater reality than the realm of the ebb and flow of everyday life. And this is accomplished, I think, essentially by two means. There is first of all the element of shock. Clowns among the Pueblos, for example, in the context of their ritual dance dramas, engage in, among other activities, types of sexual display which normally are quite taboo in such societies, and this causes a rupture with the ordinary everyday pattern of life. It does that by immediately catching the attention: it helps the people forget their petty little concerns about the routines of daily life. It shocks them out of that. Secondly, once that awareness, that alertness and openness, has been achieved through the initial shock, then it is possible to communicate on another level through the use of humor. As I see it, all this puts the mind of the person involved in a frame which relates to the humor of the situation, thus serving to open doors to a wider vista. It does this extremely effectively, because all of this takes place, as I have suggested, within a very serious ritual or dance-drama context, which involves enormous concentration, great attention to the minute details of the rites of the ceremonies that are being carried out—and the rigors of all this demand some kind of relief, some way in which what is being stated through the rites can be translated onto a much deeper level, transcending the activities, or the forms and motions of the rite itself. Thus shock and humor open into another realm. It is a very Zen-like technique, it seems to me.

P. Yes, I was just thinking of the traditional Zen master, who certainly uses the technique of shock and humor. But I have a question there: the humor is apparently very often directed toward the rite itself. It's as if the ritual solemnities were being made fun of. Now from what you say, I gather that you think this is done in order that the truth that is within these rites should be somehow put on a different level, but not destroyed; would you say the humor is not destructive, it is not *against*?

J.B. I see it as a technique to translate the formal rite or to break through it into an area of deeper meaning and deeper awareness on the part of the participant. It is you might say a shattering of the structure of the rite in order to get at the essence of the rite. It seems to ridicule, thus destroy, but it does this so that deeper truths contained within the rite can come forth and reveal themselves.

P. I wonder if you could describe some manifestations of the trickster or the clown when this role is being played?

J.B. Well, there are many examples one could take, but I always like to use those out of Plains Indian culture, out of my own experience with the so-called *Heyhokas* among the Sioux, especially among the friends I lived with in Black Elk's family, and with Black Elk himself, who was a *Heyhoka*.

P. He was? I didn't know that!

J.B. Oh, yes! In the first place, to become a *Heyhoka*, or what is sometimes called a Contrary, requires a deep spiritual experience—a very intense quality of dream, or more often a vision experience. This sacred origin is important, because it gives the key to the fact that what we are really dealing with in the activities of the *Heyhoka* is of a spiritual nature, and is a means of transmitting spiritual truths to the larger community. The quality of the vision that leads to becoming a *Heyhoka* is institution-alized in a sense, in that it has to be a vision involving certain forms or certain powers—lightning, for example. the Thunder Beings, or the dog; if one has such a vision, this requires that the person become a *Heyhoka*.

P. A vision of any one of these?

J.B. At least among the Sioux, yes. However, the strongest sign probably is of lightning, whether in the form of the Thunder Beings, or the eagle perhaps, which is associated with lightning. This was Black Elk's experi-ence, which forced him to become a trickster figure, a *Heyhoka*, one who has the obligation—and it is a very weighty function that is imposed on such a person—to do things in ways which break with the traditional norms. Sometimes the *Heyhoka*'s actions are very humorous, because this is, as we have said, a part of the technique for shattering a person's perception of, and participation in, the everyday routines of life. To break through the habitual enables one to take some distance from oneself—to see things a little bit more objectively, and thereby on a higher level. So

Black Elk

the *Heyhokas* do all sorts of strange things: they do things upside down or backwards; sometimes they will pitch a tepee with the poles on the outside of the lodge covering, with the smoke flaps facing the wrong way, or with the doorway to the west instead of to the east. When they sit in the tepee maybe they will do it upside down, with their feet up in the air, lying on their backs on the ground; and this of course makes people laugh. Normally when you enter a tepee in the Plains, you must move around it in a sunwise direction, clockwise; but the *Heyhoka* will do it the wrong way. Everything is done in reverse. Sometimes instead of going in the doorway they lift up the lodge cover at the back and crawl under; things like that. Sometimes their tricks aren't so funny. I remember one story an old Sioux woman told me, and she was really mad about it. Her husband was a *Heyhoka*, and she had just finished making a pair of decorated moccasins for him. They were in the lodge and she tossed them to him across the fire, saying, "Here, try them on." In their language, which is Lakota, that sounds very much like, "Here, burn them up," and so he picked them up and threw them into the fire, and burned up his nice new moccasins; and she was furious. She didn't think that was very funny.

P. I really can't blame her!

J.B. But maybe it did something for her, to help her to take a greater distance from her craft work. Sometimes in making things one becomes too attached to what is made, forgetting that things are never permanent!

There are hundreds of stories like that. I like the one Black Elk used to tell about the *Heyhokas* who rushed out of the tepee after a little sprinkling of rain and saw a large puddle; with great flourishes and gesticulations they took off their clothes down to the breech clout, and then they got a long pole, about twenty feet long, and laid it horizontally across the puddle, and then they set it up vertically in order to measure the depth of the water, and saw it was about twenty feet deep, you see? So with a great deal of display, making sure everybody in camp was looking, they dove into the water, which was only a few inches deep, and hit their heads hard, and made everybody laugh. And that's good, because what is life without laughter? It's very important.

P. What did Black Elk do as a *Heyhoka*?

J.B. Well, he was always doing funny things. That is why it was always good to live with him, because you never knew what to expect. Something completely unexpected that would happen when you were traveling with him, for instance. There was a time—this isn't exactly humorous, but it shows the ability of the *Heyhoka* to seize on any occasion and use it in an imaginative, unusual way. It was in Denver—which was not a very pleasant city in the early 1940s; there was a great deal of prejudice and racism, and we had a hard time finding a hotel room. When we did find one it was a very dingy, horrible room and Black Elk felt bad about Denver and the hotel; he felt unclean and he wanted a sweat bath to cleanse himself of the impurities of that city. I didn't know how this could be done in a hotel room; but the room was heated by a coal fire, and the fireplace was brick and so old the bricks were falling out of it. He said, "Here, let's take these loose bricks, and we'll pull some more out of the chimney and heat them in the coal fire," which we did. Then we took the chairs in the room and made them into a circle, and took all the bedding off the beds and laid it over the chairs to make a kind of lodge right there in the middle of the hotel room. We found an old coal scuttle and when the bricks were red hot we put them in the coal scuttle, placed that in the little lodge, and stripped down and crawled in; and it was good and hot in there and we sang and prayed and smoked and sweated and it was real good, you know? I think that was the first time a sweat bath has ever been taken in a Denver hotel room; but that is typical of the kind of thing that happens with these people. The unexpected, breaking with habitual patterns, adds a dimension to life that I think is terribly important.

P. When Black Elk was acting as a religious leader among his people, did he put aside the *Heyhoka* role?

J.B. No; it is incumbent upon the *Heyhoka* always to be a *Heyhoka*; you can't turn it on and off.

P. How did he reconcile the two roles?

J.B. The leading of serious, sacred rites isn't contrary to breaking the seriousness of those rites with humor. It gives dramatic relief; it is a universal technique. Very often, right in the middle of a sacred rite, the opening of a medicine bundle, for instance, there'll be a kind of break or recess, and at that time they'll start telling very funny stories; and in this most serious context of all suddenly everyone is laughing and rolling on the ground.

P. That reminds me of an experience of my own, when I was admitted to the preparation of a Navajo sand-painting ceremony. At the same time that the medicine man was making the sand painting, and instructing a couple of young assistants exactly how it was done, he was also making great fun of us, and there was a great deal of laughter. They would stop every now and then and say, "Thankyou thankyou thankyou!" They think it is very funny the way we say "thank you," and the laugher was uproarious. It was my first experience of Indians in action and I was very much astonished at this mixture of the solemn with ridicule.

J.B. And so often for an outsider it is very, very hard to take, because we feel offended, and so on. But if we can really stand off from ourselves and see that indeed we really *are* very funny in certain circumstances, and start to laugh at ourselves, then all of a sudden—and this I think is the point of the whole thing—something opens up and another quality of participation becomes possible. You know, in many of those cults or sects where everything is taken so very seriously and everything must be very solemn and one must never smile because a smile is against religion, one wonders—in a truly spiritual sense, what is the real work that goes on within? In many American Indian cultures, on the Northwest coast, for instance, certain rites and ceremonies can't be started until all the guests who have ben invited to participate start to laugh—open up. Once they start to laugh, then the ground is prepared for a real quality of participation in the sacred dimensions of what the rite is all about.

Sometimes—I'm thinking now again of Black Elk—the tricks backfire in tragic ways. For example, as *Heyhoka* Black Elk had the right and indeed the obligation to do things which were amazing and antinatural, and he once proclaimed that he was going to make the earth rise in front of everybody within the tepee. What he had done was to place gunpowder a few inches under the surface of the earth and then at a certain point in his ceremony, when he called on the earth to rise, he touched off the gunpowder with a cigarette or something, and indeed the earth did rise, but the flare-up from the gunpowder was too close to him and it singed his eyes; and from that time on he was very nearly completely blind. That wasn't so funny. No one else was hurt, but he always used to say that he had been punished for trying to go too far in fooling people.

There is something that I think is very important about these tricks and strange phenomena: very often it is evident to the outsider that there is some pragmatic explanation for the trick, some sleight of hand or other, and very often that is the case and the people are very aware of it. But that doesn't mean to them that the performer is a fake or a charlatan; they relate to this in a different way from the way we would—not with suspicion but with an understanding that however the phenomenon was accomplished, it illustrates the illusory nature of phenomena in general. And realizing the illusory nature of phenomena, the world of appearances, of *maya* as the Hindus would say, again helps one to break through to a reality that is more real.

P. Do you remember an article of Sam Gill's, in an early issue of PARABOLA, in which he was speaking of just that among the Hopi, with the kachinas? There is a disillusionment of the children at a certain age; they have been brought up with all sorts of Santa Claus stories about the kachinas. He also spoke about some tribes in Australia and the initiation rites for young boys, where they frighten them to death with bullroarers, keeping them blindfolded, and then suddenly the blindfolds are taken off and they see that these terrible roaring gods are their own fathers, laughing at them! He made a very interesting case for the extraordinary effect that this could have on the children, of bringing them to an entirely different level of understanding.

J.B. Right—that is what I feel is accomplished. He was writing about the kachina initiation rites of the Hopi and how after very serious rites, indeed, a terrifying display where the initiates were whipped, all of a sudden the elders take off their masks and start whipping each other and joking and the children see they are their fathers and uncles and so on. So you have again the theme of shock and then release of tension with humor, and then hopefully understanding on a deeper level which is appropriate at this particular age; they are old enough to understand the mysteries of the kachinas, but on a deeper level possible with maturity.

P. I don't succeed in understanding very well the connection here with the enormous body of Trickster myths—all the shenanigans of Coyote, for instance, combined with his semi-divinity. What is the intention there?

J.B. Yes, these tales now involve not people but animal or mythical beings who take on the role of the clown, whether it is Coyote, the Algonkin Nanabozo, the Great Hare, or the Siouan *Iktomi*, the Spider. First of all, the stories are always transmitted orally by storytellers, the elders who are often great artists, actors who are able to tell it in a way that immediately catches the attention of the children, the old people, everybody. They use all kinds of dramatic devices to hold their listeners' attention. Also the telling of these tales is always under certain circumstances: sometimes only in the winter season, as among the Navajos, after certain beings have gone underground, like bears and spiders, who have negative potentialities. Or they may only be told at nighttime; in other words, the context in which the tales are told has to be special, and that lends importance to the telling of them. Then the tales themselves are acted out, often using many theatrical devices, and most of them present things that one isn't supposed to do in everyday life—as in the Coyote tales. For example, Coyote is always complaining about his hunger; and everybody knows you should never do that. So when the moment comes when he complains of hunger, everybody laughs, because they know it is not appropriate. Or Coyote is carried away by his sex impulses, and again everybody laughs because they know that such excesses are not acceptable behavior. Of course eventually Coyote gets punished for allowing his appetites to run away with him. But a number of things happen in these tales on a number of different levels. First of all there is what you might call the moralistic level. (There is never the punch line that we have in Aesop's fables: "This is what happens if you do this"—everybody gets the point without having to emphasize it like that.) On this moralistic level, the tales set the parameters for acceptable behavior; they define the limits outside of which you are not allowed to go if you are a member of that particular cultural group. Secondly, on what seems to me a higher level of understanding, the miraculous events that are always a part of the tale instruct us that this shifting world of appearances is not really real; there are other levels of reality. For instance, Coyote is tricked into a hollow log and can't get out, nevertheless he is able to take a clamshell from behind his ear and cut his body into tiny pieces and throw them out of a knothole; then once outside he puts himself together again. Thus these episodes again help to break the

JOSEPH EPES BROWN • 177

shell of this world of appearances in which we tend to be too set. Then there is the humor too, and these together, as with the clown, open up the possibility of participation on other, deeper levels of reality. It is a *most* effective device, whether used by the clown or in the adventures of the Trickster being.

P. Are there special people who are allowed to tell stories? Do they tell them in their houses, or is there a communal storytelling? Or does this vary?

J.B. It varies a great deal. Sometimes just in the evening when the family is there, an elder is chosen, or spontaneously he begins to tell the story, or it may be a younger person who is noted for his skill in using dramatic devices. Such oral transmission is a great art form, and it is a tragedy that with the emphasis on literacy and so on it has been increasingly lost to people, with all that this implies. For these truths are the kinds of things that are transmitted only through the oral traditions. Also, for the full import of the tales they must be told in their own language.

P. Is the storytelling kept up at all in the families now?

J.B. It depends; but I suspect that with families that have been accultur- ated and have lost their own indigenous language, with the impact of television and so on, it has not been kept up. But now on many of the reservations there is a new emphasis on regaining command of their own language and establishing in their schools a curriculum in that language. This is helping, I think, to bring back these traditions and the values which they bear.
As an educator, if that is what I am in part, it seems to me there is no more effective mode of communication and education than through the person-to-person oral transmissions.
If I were to sum up what I have been trying to say about the Trickster type tales, I think the basic thing is the ambivalent character of the Trickster; he can be a rascal, and he can also be a culture hero, the one who brings the good things, the sacred things, to the people. He always has this ambivalence: he is a rascal but he is also a hero. And to me what this suggests is that this is a way of explaining the ambivalence of nature— its tricky character, its seeming reality. Phenomena seem to be real and yet

they are not. As Black Elk used to say, this world is a shadow of another, more real world—fused but not confused; dual, but not separate.

P. That's it: the relation of the two; but very often what is apparent is contradiction.

J.B. A seeming contradiction.

P. Yes; actually what is interesting is the real relation. So this is what I am trying to get at also about the Trickster and the Fool, the hero and the villain. Could you give us an example of how let's say *Iktomi,* the mischief maker and Trickster of the Sioux, appears also as a hero, or in a positive or creative form?

J.B. *Iktomi* of course among the Sioux is a Spider being—*Iktomi* in Lakota means spider. As with Coyote, the Spider is also a tricky and very clever person.

P. Is he related to the Navajo Spider Woman?

J.B. A little bit, yes, in some ways. You appreciate why the spider was chosen if you look at all the different types of spiders and what they are able to do, and how superior they are as hunters, and how the trapdoor spiders can set traps for their prey, or how spiders that build their webs in concentric circles are able to draw out of their own being two different kinds of threads, one smooth and one sticky, and how in making those webs, the threads that go in to the center are smooth but the threads that are in concentric circles are sticky; and of course it is the sticky ones that catch the prey. There is in this, you see, a positive message for the people, indeed a spiritual message: that so long as you travel to the center, you don't get stuck, trapped, eaten up; but if you go to the right or left, if you diverge from the straight way to the center, you get caught. And so this, you have to say, is a positive lesson that Spider has taught the people. Then there are all the different ways of hunting their prey that spiders use; people learn from that. They observe that certain types of spiders, when they are hatched out of their eggs, send up little filaments into the air and they are carried by the winds for great distances, like balloons; and the people see this as a certain control that the spiders have over the forces of the winds, and they would like to have themselves. So there is a whole range of positive things that one can learn from the spider. He is thought of as a very industrious person, and thus is held up as an example to young girls, because he is always working, weaving, or building. In order to make this more concrete to children, mothers used to stretch ropes and make a kind of spider web between four trees so it became a hammock, and they placed their children in the middle. The trees were situated according to the four directions of space, and the feeling was that the child would receive powers from the four directions, situated there in the center of the spider web.

P. So *Iktomi* is sometimes benevolent; he is not always the mischief maker?

J.B. No; for example, the people also look on him as a kind of culture hero who brings important and indeed sacred things to the people—the Sioux, for instance, have a belief that they have never made their own arrowheads out of flint. They find them on the prairie, beautifully made; and the belief is that they were made by *Iktomi*, by the Spider, and this is his offering to the people. It is something valuable, something good; the flint arrow-point is very sacred, in part because of the association of flint with fire and lightning.

P. But is it true that they don't make arrow points?

J.B. As far as I know; I have never met a Sioux who knew how to chip an arrowhead out of flint. And their answer is, "Well, we never had to; the Spider did it for us and we find them in little piles on the prairie and we just pick them up."

P. How extraordinary!

J.B. On the other hand, as we have said, Spider can be very, very tricky. This is why sometimes a white person is called an *Iktomi*, because they are smart, you know, and can be very tricky, and you don't know what they are going to do next; and you have to be careful. Sometimes FBI agents are called *Iktomis*—if they aren't called *igamoos*, which means cat.

P. Is that even worse?

J.B. It's a little more derogatory!

P. What more could you tell us about Black Elk?

J.B. Well, just that as a *Heyhoka*, a sometimes clown figure, he liked to make people laugh; he felt happy when people were laughing. When there were any little children around he would always be doing funny things with them or telling them funny stories, to make them laugh. I think he understood that there is no access to a deeper spiritual reality if there is not the opening force of laughter present there. It tends to open the heart for receiving a greater value than that of this world. That is why it was always a happy experience to be with him, in spite of the fact that in many moments of his life he was a very sad, tragic figure, because of his feeling that he had never been able to bring to reality the task that had been imposed on him through his visions—to mend the hoop of his nation, to bring his people together and have the tree of his culture flourish again. He always felt he had failed in that mission. So he was sad; and on the other hand (and this is typical of the dual nature of the *Heyhoka*) he loved to laugh and to make other people laugh.

P. Can you tell us anything about his death? Were you there when he died?

J.B. No, I wasn't; I was in Europe then. It is interesting that Black Elk always said: "You will know when I am dying, because there will be a great display of some sort in the sky." And it was true; in Europe I didn't see it, but in talking with people on the Pine Ridge Reservation, they said the sky was filled with falling stars at the time of his death—a very unusual display.

P. Was there any special ritual of becoming a *Heyhoka*—a kind of initiation?

J.B. Normally when an intense vision experience came to a person, he would be required to act it out or paint some aspect of it, or display it in a dance.

P. Then do these dances become a part of the public ritual? Are they repeated afterward?

J.B. Yes, sometimes. But normally the particular enactment is specific to that person so long as he is living, and usually no other person would have the right to perform it.

P. His songs also are his, and not be be sung by anyone else?

J.B. Sacred songs are usually very personal and very private, and no one else sings them. In many Indian cultures such songs are considered as private property. On the Northwest coast this is true, for there songs are a kind of commodity; they can be sold to someone else who thereby has the right to sing them. It is the same way with personal sacred names—they can be bought sometimes. If you can come up with enough cowrie shells, or cedar boxes or whatever it is, to acquire the power of that name or song, you have the right to do so.

You see, we look on these things out of our usual attitudes towards buying and selling. One has to start thinking in other ways in order to understand some of these things that don't seem important to us. For instance, and as we have discussed already, in our culture seriousness is associated with religious activity, whereas here we are talking about cultures that insist on laughter as being integral and appropriate to sacred experience; this is what could be called institutionalized humor, for we are not talking about just telling bawdy jokes as might take place in a bar. Such institutionalized humor, always used in a manner appropriate to the time or the circumstance, seems to occur across many religious traditions. You could make a case for the same sort of thing in Zen; you can find it in Islam, for example, in the exploits of Mullah Nassr Eddin, or among the "People of Blame," as they are called, who do all sorts of strange things in order to hide their true spiritual state. They may dress in strange ways, do things backward or upside down; and those who follow the conventional pattern are shocked by this, but perhaps it does them good to be shook up a little bit. You see, the people who do these things in such strange ways may be very holy men; they are often the real spiritual leaders.

The most sacred is often hidden in strange ways, and I think there is a very great wisdom concealed behind some of the Native American forms and practices. But at the same time, these same forms and practices could reveal that wisdom to us, if we could understand. And there are many things here we very much need to understand.

13

◆

A Conversation between P.L. Travers and Laurens van der Post

"Dreams and Seeing," VOL. VII:2, May, 1982

Where Will All
the Stories Go?

*T*he following conversation—or as P.L. Travers calls it, a *"coming together"—took place between two lovers and guardians of story: African-born Laurens van der Post and Australian-born P.L. Travers. Sir Laurens, knighted by Her Majesty in recognition of his distinguished career as a writer, soldier, and explorer, is the author of many books, including* Venture into the Interior, Heart of the Hunter, The Dark Eye in Africa, *and* Bar of Shadow. *His fields of expertise are many and varied, and his friendships and enthusiasms have a wide range—from the Bushmen who influenced his childhood and whom he later sought out and celebrated in his famous book* Lost World of the Kalahari, *to C.G. Jung, whose close friend he became in Jung's later years. P.L. Travers, O.B.E., world-famed storyteller & creator of* Mary Poppins, *is the author also of* Friend Monkey, About the Sleeping Beauty, The Fox in the Manger, *and* Two Pairs of Shoes.

♦

P.L. TRAVERS Laurens, let us go back to the beginning of things. I have long carried this question—where, having come so far, will all the stories go? Naturally, since it is your country, I am thinking specially of Africa. And I wonder, when everyone there has a television set, what will happen to the ancient lore? Only today I was reading of the increasing

185

number of suicides among those who leave the wild for the cities. Lacking the extended family, separated from the tribe, and therefore from the stories, what have they to lean upon? Already the stories are becoming unavailable to those who need them most. Well, you know more about this than anyone, almost, in the world. Let us share it together.

LAURENS VAN DER POST Ah, I do not believe that I know more about stories than you do, but I couldn't love them more. And I love them because it seems to me that without the stories, human beings wouldn't be here. Couldn't be. Human beings *are* a story; they are living a story and anyone open to this story is living a part—perhaps all—of themselves.

P.L.T. So there is no need to invent myths, which is what—feeling a lack in themselves—people are nowadays trying to do?

L.v.d.P. Well, I think that that is an impossibility. It is one of the great illusions of the literature and the art and the life of our time that people like Tolkien are supposed to have "invented" myths. They have done nothing of the sort. They have substituted a sort of intellectual effort, a conscious determination—which they, quite wrongly, call myth—for this very profound process which cannot come from anywhere but out of life itself. It is something that falls into us. I have been very much concerned about this because, only recently, I was asked to say something about Descartes' famous statement—"I think, therefore I am." *There*, it seems to me, is the beginning of the fatal hubris of our time. Of course, there is an area in which we think—who could deny it?—but, really, all the most important aspects of thought come from that which is thinking through us. And this process is the myth, one of the most profound things of life; it is creation itself, which becomes accessible, and, in part, energizes and gives, of its own accord, a sense of direction to the human creature. It is something with which—if we use our brains and imagination—we are in partnership. And the story is one of the roots of this area, this area from which the myth arises, which sustains and feeds the human spirit and enables man, and life on earth, to be greater than it could otherwise have been.

P.L.T. And that's what men are now hunting for—for life's sake, one could say—and they think they can get it by inventing the kind of thing that brought *Roots* to all the television screens in America.

L.V.D.P. What makes it so sad is that it comes out of the genuine longing of millions of people for roots, those millions who do not realize that in the most profound sense, we carry our roots within ourselves. They need not be physical roots, which is what this man has tried to provide, a phony kind of physical source for what, in a sense, is the super-physical, a hunger for roots in the myth.

P.L.T. I would say that really we don't even need that "super." It exists. It courses in our blood, carried along from one generation to the next— wouldn't you agree?

L.V.D.P. I would. I only use the word "super" as a substitute for the whole process which moves and works within us.

P.L.T. It's the same with the word "supernatural." For me, the natural includes the "super." And this brings us to what you wrote in, I think, *The Heart of the Hunter*, where you say—or, rather, the Bushmen say— "We are dreamed by a dream."

L.V.D.P. Ah, I was very moved by that because, being in the company of a very ancient form of man, a Stone Age hunter in the Kalahari Desert, I was pressing him to tell me about the Beginning, *his* idea of the Beginning and the beginning of those stories you were speaking of. He looked at me in astonishment and said, "Well, that's a very difficult thing because, you must know, there's a dream dreaming us." And this seemed to me to sum it up, to arrive, for instance, at the point where all the explorers of the human spirit have begun—and also ended. It leads us to Shakespeare's famous conclusion in *The Tempest*, where he comes face to face with the fact that he has exhausted all his own powers, come to the frontiers of himself, where something other than what has brought him to this point must now carry him on. You remember the epilogue—

And my ending is despair
Unless I be relieved by prayer. . . .

But even before that he has come to the conclusion that

We are such stuff
As dreams are made on.

And what is the distance between him and that little Stone Age man who had never before seen a white man and never heard of Shakespeare? For his own myth inside him tells him: "Look out! Watch! Listen! A dream is dreaming through you." And this enriches him. It seems to me that this man, whom everybody else thought of as poor, despised, rejected, was rich in a way that we, with our technological abundance, are destitute.

P.L.T. We have nothing, we are poverty-stricken. This, in a way, is like the Australian concept of the Dreaming, of which I know a little, having been brought up there. Everything that is not at this very instant—when we're chopping wood or finding witchetty grubs—is in the Dreaming. I can go into the Dreaming and you can go into the Dreaming at any moment and be refreshed. The anthropologists call it the Dreamtime but that word "time" immediately makes things move serially, puts them into place and locality. The Aborigines speak of it as the Dreaming—in their tribal tongues, *Yamminga* or *Dooghoor*—and for them everything is there. It is similar to what Celtic peoples mythically call the Cauldron. They cannot go further back in their thought than a great-grandfather, nor further forward than a great-grandson. Beyond these, all is in the Dreaming—the making of the world, the great days, the great heroes. I was reminded of all this when reading—oh, it comes in several of your books—of what you—or the Bushmen, rather—call "tapping." "There is a tapping in me." Perhaps if Tolkien and the makers of *Roots* and all the other inventors of what cannot be invented could hear that tapping, listen for it as your Bushmen do, it could be in them as well, don't you think?

L.v.d.P. Yes. It is very interesting that we have both instinctively picked on Tolkien, because—though few realize it—Tolkien himself was born in Bushman country—at a place I know very well. And his own journey, his particular inward journey, began when, as a boy of eight, he had a vision of the evening star in the sky over Africa, that part of Africa which was ancient Bushman country. And to that extent he was sustained. It was those first eight African years that impelled him on his journey and aroused in him a sense of the importance of myth; but not sufficiently strongly for him to approach the myth in a spirit of humility, in the sense that he could have laid himself down and said: "Take over. Tell me what you're about." Instead, he began telling the myth what *it* was about and so, of course, it's no longer mythology. It doesn't work.

P.L.T. It remains invention. It comes out of his own enthusiasm and not from the myth's requirement.

L.v.d.P. It is the same process which has made modern man speak of this organic, dynamic force in the human spirit as unreal. They use myth as a synonym of that which is not.

P.L.T. As synonymous with lie. I am constantly protesting against that. What would Mantis say, I wonder, Mantis who is one of the great embodiments of myth that you write of so often and that I remember, too, from childhood. For me she was simply a praying mantis, I did not know her as a mythical creature. But she filled me with a sense of wonder—the long narrow-waisted insect praying. I would stand for hours watching her, wondering when the prayer would end. But it never did. The saints must envy such energy! And then, when I grew up, I found Mantis in your books and knew her—or him?—for one of the Lordly Ones. Tell a little about that.

L.v.d.P. Well, it's almost impossible for me to see Mantis apart from my own beginning because of my early experience. One of the great influences in my life was a Stone Age nurse, far more important to me than my own parents. I remember, as a little boy, hearing her talking with Mantis. She was asking, in the Bushman tongue, "How high is the water?" And the mantis would put down its tiny hands.

P.L.T. You actually saw the mantis doing this? It is so completely a ritual.

L.v.d.P. I saw the mantis doing this. And I protested to my nurse, "But, look, we're not near any water. We're a thousand miles from the sea. Why do you talk to Mantis about water? Does water come out of the desert?" "Well," she said, "in the beginning, water was everywhere and Mantis was nearly drowned. And a bee came and rescued him and flew all day long till the sun began to go down. Then the bee looked desperately round for a place where it could put Mantis and, suddenly, there it was! A wonderful flower above the water, a flower we no longer see on this earth, and the bee put Mantis inside it. So Mantis was safe, for from there, under the power of his own wings, he could find a dry rock to sit on."

P.L.T. Ah, the bee! It had to be in the story, the sacred creature that everywhere brings and symbolizes life. Do you remember how the bees stung you and tried to send you away from the place of the sacred tree, so that your presence should not profane it? You first saw it in the swamp, remember, then in your dream, and again among those mysterious rocks that would not have their photographs taken. The bee was there, in that place of magic, where the paintings refused to go into the camera.

L.v.d.P. This is one of the strangest things that ever happened to me and it continues to haunt me. It's as though there's a parable in it, for, at that moment, not only myself, but the people for whom I was responsible, were in very grave danger. We were in a great treacherous swamp and one of my paddlers—we were using dugouts—was Samutchoso, a name meaning "That which is left after reaping"—I didn't know that he was the so-called witch-doctor of my dugout people, the Makoros—and he said to me: "There's something I ought to tell you. Out there in the desert there are some hills and in these hills, right inside them, there are many rooms, and in these rooms live the master spirits of all created life. And on top of these hills, there's a pool of water that has never yet dried up; and beside this pool there is a tree whose name we not only do not know, but are not allowed to try to know, a tree that has fruit on it and this fruit is the fruit of knowledge." "Why are you telling me this?" I asked. "Ah," he said, "that is for *you* to say." "Well, if we get out of this alive," I said, "will you take me there?" "Yes, I will," he said, "but on one condition— that on the way to the hills there is no shooting, no killing. It's a law of their spirits—they are called the Slippery Hills, the Tsoudilo Hills—that no one may come to them with blood on his hands."

I solemnly agreed.

Well, it so happened that I had a great deal of trouble getting out of the swamp and after that many difficulties to face. But when, many months later, I was free to go back, I myself remembered my pledge but, alas, I forgot to share it with the people who were traveling with me. So, on the way to the hills, with Samutchoso guiding us—I, as always, in the rear, for in the desert that is where trouble starts—one of those in front sighted a buck and, knowing that we needed food, shot it. I went cold when I heard those shots ring out and, seeing the expression on Samutchoso's face, I said to myself, "Pray God, they've missed!" and to Samutchoso, "Forgive me. Don't blame them. I forgot to tell them." "It's not for me to forgive," he said. "Only the spirits can do that."

When we caught up with the others we found that, unfortunately, they had not missed but had killed two animals. And, when we eventually got to the hills, rising so extraordinarily out of the desert, we were in trouble from the moment we arrived. All night, with our camps pitched at the foot of the hills, hyenas and jackals and carrion crows cried like creatures out of *The Valkyrie*. But when my mechanic, who was also my tape-recordist, tried to record those noises, the machine—we had very primitive equipment but the best that could then be had—simply wouldn't work. It had been all right before, but now we could get nothing from it. And then, at dawn, just as we were waking, we were suddenly attacked by hordes of bees, coming from all directions. One of my guides, on all my Kalahari journeys, a marvelous and blameless man who had been for three years in the desert with me, got forty-three stings and was very ill. Curiously enough, I, alone, was not stung. And the moment the sun rose, all the bees vanished. So, we set out to start filming on the way. Looming above the desert, we came across a large rock and on it a set of rock paintings which no European had ever seen. "Film!" I shouted, and the camera started to turn. Then, suddenly, it snapped! It wouldn't work. The photographer inserted another magazine. Again the thing started turning and again it snapped and went out. So it continued all the morning, magazine after magazine not working and, as a last straw, the pivot on which the magazine turned—it was a fine German Araflex camera—disintegrated. Imagine it—a thing of steel! We were now without a camera but I still have in my possession such reels as we could save and it's extraordinary how the shots start in frame, then gradually the frame narrows and—then stops.

"Well, at least," I said to Samutchoso, "you could, perhaps, take us to that pool that is never without water!"

In silence he led us on, past what must have been an ancient temple of some sort, for all the way to the top of the hills the rocks were embellished with most marvelous paintings—thousands of them, as though the animals they depicted were leading us in procession towards the pool, to keep us company. Thus it was we arrived at the water and beside it the tree with the strange fruit on it and a rock in which could clearly be seen two deep indentations.

"Here," said Samutchoso, "is the place where the first spirit knelt when he prayed to the tree to take care of all that had been created. I will show you how he prayed." And he knelt down in the two marks and was about to raise his hands in prayer, when he fell back, shocked, his face ashen. "The spirits have tried to kill me," he cried, and hurried us away, back to the camp, not permitting us to pluck any of the fruit in order that it could be identified. "No! We are not allowed to take it," he said. "The spirits are very angry." That night, the recorder again refused to work and the next day we were again assailed by bees. We were all of us in such a state about this that I even began to wonder whether my Land Rover could be persuaded to start. For three days we tried to get camera and recorder working—nothing doing, nothing.

P.L.T. Man's work. Man's work. It failed because something more powerful had taken over.

L.v.d.P. Yes. And I was at my wits' end. So I walked out, in the evening, to be on my own, taking my gun—it was dangerous country—simply for protection. I walked for miles round the base of the hills and suddenly, out of them, stepped an enormous Kudu bull, a marvelous animal; it really looked to me like a god, in the level light of the sun. I looked at it and it looked back at me, absolutely without fear, as though in that look it was trying to tell me something. I was so moved by this that I gave it a military salute; and it turned around and went into the bush and away back up the hill.

As I returned to camp, something happened in me that made me say to Samutchoso—"Suppose I wrote a letter to the spirits asking forgiveness and buried it at the foot of the first rock picture—a pair of hands impressed in paint on the rock—do you think that would help?" In reply, he took a needle, asked me for a piece of cotton which he wound round his hand, then, putting the needle in the lifeline of his left hand, he gazed at it in a sort of trance. And suddenly it seemed as though he were seeing millions of beings around him, for he murmured to them, "No, no, not you! Nor you, nor you, but *you over there*, come here to me." Apparently, whatever it was obeyed, for he communed with it for a long time and then came out of his trance, saying: "Yes, I think it might work, but the spirits are very angry with you."

I felt in my bones that this letter would need to be correct in every detail—even with place and time and date and a map reference as well. So I wrote, asking forgiveness for any unintentional disrespect we had shown, saying that this letter was an act of contrition not only on our own behalf but on that of others who might come after us. I made everybody sign it and those who could not, made their mark.

"Really, Laurens," said my hunter—a great friend and terribly English— "this is too ridiculous! I simply can't do a thing like this! What if they hear of it at my club?" But he signed, nevertheless, and I promised that the club would never know. So we rinsed out an old bottle, put the letter inside, and securely corked it, and Samutchoso and I went out at dawn and buried it at the foot of the hill. A feeling of some kind of catharsis came over me then, and I said to Samutchoso—"You brought us here. Can you tell me if it will be all right to take us back?" "It's not for me to say. You must ask the spirits." And again he went through his motions with the needle. "The spirits say that all will be well now, but at this place to which you are going—(I did not myself know, at the time, where we were going)—you will meet more trouble. You must realize, however, that it belongs to the past."

Then, as we walked back he said sadly, even tragically, "You know, even ten years ago, if you'd offended them like this, you would now, quite surely, be dead. They are not what they were, the spirits."

P.L.T. They are not what they were because man is not what he was! Though I couldn't help feeling a little kindly towards the hunter who was afraid the club might get to hear of it! That spirits could read an English letter and the marks of untutored men—who would believe that? It takes an acquaintance with myth to recognize that what you did was an outward and visible sign of an inward and spiritual intention.

L.v.d.P. Yes. And there's a sequel. People now know from my books about this letter and the place where it was buried, and fly aircraft overhead to try to get a glimpse of the paintings. Immediately after my experience a German scientific expedition went to investigate them, and barged in with their trucks which were immediately destroyed by fire. So, it's not just subjective. There is also objective evidence. And yet, knowing all this, and the spirit in which I had done it, they have dug up the bottle and it's now in the museum at Botswana. That's where the myth is, in museums, for most of us.

P.L.T. Sacrilege. And I asked you where the stories go! I can't ask what we can do to get them back but know only that it has to be done. There must be a few men who understand the need for this. For instance, not long ago, I was told of three or four English doctors who had gone out to live with some African tribe to learn their methods of healing; and how they discovered that this is not a matter of giving a medicine or an antidote to one person, but that it is, rather, a communal matter—the whole family, the whole tribe, is concerned with the healing; feasting, dancing, sharing the sickness and health among all. How could we bring such an activity to our world—such sharedness? But perhaps something has started.

L.v.d.P. Well, I think you must just go on telling stories. They, too, are under law and cannot escape from it.

P.L.T. You mean, perhaps, that, ultimately, the stories themselves can heal?

L.v.d.P. Yes, that is probably a more accurate way of saying it. This process cannot be defeated: life itself depends on it. I could tell you so many examples from the primitive world.

P.L.T. Well, tell me about the one—because I have something to add to it—where the Bushman woman came down on a cord and promised to stay with her Bushman husband as long as he did not look into her basket.

L.v.d.P. Yes, that story is much to the point. Stories of the stars play a fantastic role in their lives, if you know how to decode them. You touch the spirit of Greece here. The Bushman's origin of the Milky Way is very like the Greek. I once saw a Bushman woman holding up her child to the sky and asking that it be given the heart of a star.

P.L.T. I have thought that that's where Haley got his scene where the child is held up to the moon—from your Bushman story.

L.V.D.P. Well, you probably know as well as I do the enormous amount of borrowing that goes on in the modern world.

P.L.T. Ah, but, you know, it has to be, this borrowing. It's not yours or mine. It's there to be taken, a great big cauldron. One man takes something from it, another sees this and says "That's true, that's what I want." So he goes and takes it from the first man. I'm not worried about this, it's part of the general heritage.

L.V.D.P. Yes. It's only the miserable ego that steps in. In the Bushman story the child was to have the heart of a star because "the stars," they say, "are great hunters. You can hear them on their courses up there." And that hunting, as you know, is a symbol of the search for the story, for meaning. Baudelaire talks about art being the summons on the horn of the hunter. *"Les chasseurs perdus, dans les grands bois."* Lost in the great forest of life, they blast out the summons which is art, which is story.

P.L.T. As a child in Australia, the stars seemed so close. I used to think I could hear them humming. I never told anyone, they would have laughed.

L.V.D.P. But you do. You do hear them hum. "Listen," my Bushmen would say, "they are hunting." But to get back to the story of the woman with the basket; it carries an immense mythological charge. The man, after feeling somehow that something was stolen from him, saw one night a group of beautiful girls coming down from the sky on a cord. Each carried a little tightly woven basket. And one of them, he caught. "Yes," she said, "I will live with you, on condition that you never look inside my basket without my permission." He agreed, but, inevitably, he said "What the hell!" or the Stone Age equivalent of the phrase. And one day, when he was alone, he opened the basket, peeped inside and roared with laughter. "You have looked into the basket!" she accused him, when she returned. "Yes, you silly woman, why make such a secret of it when there is nothing in it. The basket's empty." "You see *nothing*?" She gave him a tragic look, turned her back and disappeared into the sunset. And the Bushman who told me the story said to me, "It wasn't the looking but the fact that he could not perceive in the basket all the wonders she had brought him from the stars." And that, for me, in a sense is one of the images that the story is to the human spirit. The basket brings us its star-stuff and the pundits—the intellectuals and the critics—look into it and say it's all rubbish and superstition, and that there's nothing in it.

P.L.T. Would you accept a carpetbag coming from the stars? I had never read your story, but when Mary Poppins arrived, the children looked into her carpetbag and, like your Bushman, found it empty. And yet out of it came all her mundane daily possessions, including a camp bed! Did all that come from the stars? We do not know. Emptiness is fullness.

L.v.d.P. It is, it is. And I think the use of a carpetbag is a wonderful example of what I mean by making a traditional story contemporary. That carpetbag had, in fact, a magic carpet inside.

P.L.T. Yes, but disguised. And from where was the magic carpet stolen? Out of the cauldron, of course! For instance, your film on the Kalahari gave me the ostrich egg, which also must have come from there. The ostrich was such a forgetful bird, you said, that she had to put one egg in front of her outside the nest to remind her of what she was doing. Later, when I was listening to the Greek Easter service on the radio, a reporter described the monks filing in, with eyes downcast, all except one, who was gazing round at the congregation. "Clearly," said the reporter, "he had forgotten the ostrich egg hanging over the altar." But how, I wondered, had the ostrich egg gotten there? I sensed a myth in the air.

Years later, seeing a group of Coptic churches on television, all with ostrich eggs strung across the ceiling, my question arose again. I wrote to the producer, who told me that there were two schools of thought here, one that says the ostrich is a forgetful bird and another that of all the birds she is the most remembering. So, does she remember or does she forget? It almost doesn't matter. The egg, in both cases, is the reminder, and the link between my three experiences.

L.v.d.P. Yes, yes, the link. However much we try to deny it, the dream goes dreaming through us. Deep in the spirit of European man there is an ostrich and it lives heraldically. Our Prince of Wales has three ostrich feathers in his crest; in Stone Age mythology, the moon was made out of the feather of an ostrich. So the ostrich, in a sense, is Prometheus, the bird from which man, Mantis and the god-hero stole the fire and brought it to man.

P.L.T. But there's a sequel to my egg story. Hearing it, a Jungian analyst we both know gave me an ostrich egg to take with me to America. And while I was there it sat on my bookshelf, sometimes but, alas, not always, remembered. And when I was leaving for England, it seemed to me that it said "Don't take me!" So I gave it to the Dean of the Cathedral Church of St. John the Divine in New York who thought it would look well on his mantelpiece. But I knew it wouldn't stay there. The egg would go where it belonged. And it did. The next time I saw it, on another trip, it was hanging in the Cathedral, above the altar of St. Saviour's Chapel. There's a story for you!

L.v.d.P. And add to it the belief of many primitive people in Africa that the sun is an egg.

P.L.T. Is it known by whom or what it was laid?

L.v.d.P. It hatches great birds! And how it was laid is not to be known. You will find this determination among instinctive people not to try to carry an act of knowing too far. They say, "This is where we must stop." And then they let the myth take over and wait till it tells them what else there is.

P.L.T. That is what I've always found. We must stand in front of the mystery. "Take upon us," as Lear said, "the mystery of things as if we were God's spies."

L.v.d.P. Yes, and if one looks at it that way, one finds the lines of communication between the storyteller of today and the first storyteller; between us and the person who dreams, or is dreamed by the universe, these lines of communication are intact. They can never, never fail.

P.L.T. We have ancestors.

L.v.d.P. We have ancestors. Long ago I sat at the feet of a Japanese storyteller and he began with "Once Upon a Time." And years later, in a night of great turmoil, the expression on his face when he said those words came back to me.

P.L.T. The old phrase! Everywhere!

L.v.d.P. And hearing it, a great peace came upon me. I was beyond space and time, everybody was a neighbor—this universal feeling of propinquity which makes the mystics speak of the forever which is now.

P.L.T. And it will be along these lines, remembering the long genealogical tree, would you say, that we'll preserve them?

L.v.d.P. Very good, very good—Yes, through this world of ancestors, this genealogical tree of the spirit and the myth, the material of the so-called barbarians. Cafavy, one of the most civilized of modern poets, wrote:

And now what will become of us without barbarians?
Those people were some sort of a solution.

P.L.T. Let them be blest, the barbarians, and not vanish from the world!

14

♦

An Interview with Michel de Salzmann

"Guilt," VOL. VIII:1, January, 1983

The Search for Lucidity

Dr. Michel de Salzmann is concerned, as he said in a talk given in California in 1975, with both psychotherapy and the sacred. "Generally speaking I would call them both schools of self-knowledge," he said. Both "originated from the need to . . . answer our central existential question, 'Who am I?' " But he goes on to say that "though they answer the same need, I consider they should not be confused, especially if we realize they are operating on two different levels."*

Michel de Salzmann was trained in medicine, neurology, and psychiatry at the University of Paris in the years following World War II. Since then he has been practicing privately and in hospitals in Paris, and has also traveled extensively in many obscure parts of the globe studying and investigating at first hand traditional spiritual teachings as well as more modern growth techniques. Besides the fields of religion, philosophy, and science, his wide-ranging pursuits include musicology, skiing, many crafts, ancient and modern art, and the education—in its truest sense of leading forth—of the younger generation. He has made several expeditions with groups of adolescents to the Near and Middle East, and to Mt. Athos in Greece and the megalithic centers in Brittany, where the young people could come in contact with the surviving remnants of ancient religions and knowledge. Every summer in Switzerland he conducts international workshops and seminars in practical work on self-knowledge for adults, adolescents, and children.

*Jacob Needleman and Dennis Lewis, ed., *On the Way to Self Knowledge*. New York: Knopf, 1976.

202 • Leaning on the Moment

The book-lined office in which Dr. de Salzmann greeted us reminded us less of a psychiatrist's consulting room than what used to be called a "study." It is the living-working room of a man who is at once very serious about research and deeply concerned with people; the fireplace, leather chairs, the floor-to-ceiling bookshelves (very orderly) and the big desk (extremely messy) create an atmosphere that matches the man himself, with his great gravity and great charm. It is impossible not to feel his vitality, and his warmth, which at the same time is quite impersonal, as if he cared so intensely about life that people became interesting because, for a time, they contain it.

◆

PARABOLA There have been big changes in our ideas during this century, and notably in the concept of guilt. How would you approach that?

MICHEL DE SALZMANN Of course the idea of change refers us also, implicitly, to something that does not change. The concept of guilt carries various insights and connotations that certainly need to be sorted out.

I think one should start by acknowledging that throughout history, guilt is, above all, the actual fact of law transgression. It is of central importance to start with that approach, since law embodies the conceptions and principles that regulate the life and the meaning of a society and, in a way, has made us what we are.

In traditional societies, law is considered to originate from above and its violation means profanation; that is, it impedes the circulation of the sacred within the body of the community. Of course we don't point out the atrocities which, today, the degradation and imperialistic application of such a perspective have led to. In contrast, for the "primitive" mind the indivisible community works essentially as a medium between the sacred and the individual, and any fault or alienation is seen as a cellular symptom of a social disease which requires specific readjustment of the group in order to restore its fundamental function. The individual in this "primitive" society is supported by—and integrated into—an all-embracing network of significations.

P. This seems far from our personal guilt feelings.

M. de S. Yes, indeed—in such a perspective guilt is much more objectified. Our modern mind has originated from, or at least been decisively conditioned by, the split between the spiritual and the temporal, which has induced dualistic and therefore materialistic attitudes; and now it finds itself plunged into a fragmented world where it feels alone and overwhelmed by the challenge of putting all the pieces together. Individualism and its related sense of freedom is the very heavy tribute we have to pay for this fragmentation, since the individual becomes at the same time overburdened with responsibility. Existentialism, for instance, is a heart-rending echo of this situation and centers the human problem precisely around freedom, choice, responsibility, consciousness, and anxiety.

The problem of guilt, as I see it, has progressively shifted from a factual approach to a subjective problem relating, perhaps too much, to the inner "economy" of the individual. Today, guilt is much more related to what we *think* is reprehensible than to what *is* in fact reprehensible, if you see what I mean.

P. Do you regret that?

M. de S. There is no use regretting it. We have to deal with our situation as it is. The point is to try to understand it in order to be able to move towards what appears more real. Just a few minutes ago, for instance, my hastily expressed shortcut through history was so abrupt that I realize it has not conveyed properly what I had in mind, and will inevitably be misleading; yet it is done. I am factually and objectively "guilty," but I may try to do better now. I am probably too modern to follow the example of Vatel, a celebrated cook in the time of Louis XIV, who killed himself because of an unsuccessful sauce, or that of the samurai, who, in the event of a serious failure would consider hara-kiri. We should understand, however, the point of view that made it so important in older days not to "lose face." This face is not "personal" in the restricted sense we usually give this word; it is the actual function or role through which an individual is led, through serving something, to find his significance, his share, his relation to the world he belongs to.

We cannot understand ourselves outside our relation to something. And we desperately need to find our true relation toward things outside and inside ourselves, to find order and justice through discovering reality. This happens when we are aware of ourselves here and now, aware of actual "functioning." The great significance of Watergate, quite beyond the political scene, is that it reminds us that the function is, in a way, prior to the individual; it is really what creates him. And here we should not despise the alarm signal that guilt feelings represent, since they help us remember there is something greater than our ego-centered world.

P. We have to come to that. But is it not the psychological view today that guilt is an unnecessary burden, something to be gotten rid of?

M. de S. There are people who apparently don't seem to feel guilt, and others in whom it reaches a highly pathological level. One must not forget that it is the study of extreme cases, including neuroses and psychoses, which made it possible for psychoanalysis to elaborate its explanatory system of the functioning of the so-called normal man. And thanks to psychoanalysis, we are much more capable today of understanding the extent to which feelings of guilt can be destructive. We all know that self-accusation can engender such a depreciation of ourselves that we feel ourselves completely annihilated, emptied, inhibited even in our most elementary functions, without appetite, without desire, as if having forfeited the right to existence. For most of us, no accusation coming from the outside could ever have the devastating power of self-accusation. It is only in the little child that similar stresses can be observed, linked to fear and dependence with regard to the almighty adult. In guilt we relive this very same situation; we regress to an infantile state in which we feel ourselves powerless in front of a dominating and punitive inner "agency."

P. Where is the anxiety linked to guilt supposed to come from?

M. de S. Guilt would remain a simple problem if it were always appropriate to the situation, as it often is or seems to be in normal behavior. Everybody could easily understand that I may have a painful perception of having betrayed my ideals or some explicit moral law. But it becomes more complicated when the reason invoked seems inadequate, if not totally absurd, as is often the case in neuroses and psychoses. Moreover, the problem will appear insoluble when there seems to be no reason at all for guilt, when it presents itself as a diffuse feeling of unworthiness with no reference to a precise action or motivation. Freud's great achievement was to shed light on that enigma through demonstrating the fact of repression and the various mechanisms related to the unconscious. I am using the term "unconscious" here more as an adjective than as the designation for an independent or "topical" system; it qualifies the id and partly the ego and super-ego.

One can often observe in delinquents that a sense of guilt does not follow the misdemeanor, but precedes it, constituting somehow its deep motive; as though the youngster found relief in finding a justification, a real object for his guilt feelings. Likewise in neurotic behavior, guilt appears as an unconscious system of motivation which leads to and explains all kinds of sufferings that the subject inflicts on himself in a more or less spectacular and symbolic form. Failure-behavior is, for instance, an illustration of this compulsion to self-punishment. The psychoanalytic view is that all guilt problems originate from the Oedipus complex, and that pathological or behavioral types are characterized by a specific position in relation to this triangle. If not resolved in a satisfactory way it continues to manifest its pathogenic action. Anxiety is mainly related to the threat of castration—including all its symbolic equivalents—which has from the beginning motivated repression.

P. It seems that the classical psychoanalytical perspective is losing ground today, especially in the United States. Are there new trends that tend to cover it up or move away from it?

M. de S. It is true that even though it contains broader intuitions which we did not speak about, such as Eros and Thanatos, one does not get an "oceanic" impression from it but rather that of wading in a closed pool. It has a taste of prison. One can understand that some of Freud's direct disciples like Jung felt the need to open the doors in order to enlarge the perspective and situate the problem beyond the limits of individual and cultural consciousness.

According to Jung, there is a collective consciousness, beyond our individual memory, representing an immense potential from which we can draw force and meaning. The unconscious for Jung is not a residue of consciousness (as it is, in part, according to the psychoanalytic theory of repression) but the matrix of consciousness. The "self" in his perspective is the center of the total psyche—including the unconscious and consciousness—and from it emerges the ego, which becomes the center of a developing consciousness. Through consciousness there is actualized a continuing process of maturation, of "individuation"–making possible both differentiation (or uniqueness) of the person and recognition of its fundamental collective make-up—when the ego is aware of a purpose of its own that is embedded in the unconscious. If the ego is properly aware of the values and messages that are sent to it by this "Great Mother," which is the unconscious—notably through dreams and various other means—it can realize a powerful and meaningful creativity. Absence of communication, discordance between self and ego, will inevitably create indicative symptoms, which it is important to respect and listen to for a readjustment to inner harmony. Guilt is therefore a symptom related to ego betrayal of self values. Recognized as such, it may further the individuation process— together with the help of mediation and other daily spiritual practice—and can lead to seeing one's place in the universe and to take part in a larger accomplishment.

Likewise existential thinkers and analysts criticize psychoanalysis for neglecting ontology and the problems of conscience and self-consciousness. Guilt, when close to anxiety, has to be acknowledged, accepted, and "practiced" in order to fill the gap between "where we are now" and "where we want to be," without indulging in day-dreaming. When not appropriate to the situation, anxiety is neurotic and leads to psychosomatic symptoms because of repression. When it is appropriate to a threat and does not involve repression but active attitudes and awareness, its very tension becomes a source of creativity.

I think one might say that there is a unanimous agreement in psychology today that the real pathogenic factor in our conflicts is repression, however it is conceived of. This also means that the only breakthrough is consciousness. And consciousness leads to reparation, which is universally recognized as the unique specific medicine for guilt feelings.

p. How do you reconcile psychoanalytical views and views of a spiritual order, such as those you seem to have?

M. de S. They are concerned, in my opinion, with different levels. Psychoanalysis, as I approach it, is above all an access to autonomy, and to adulthood, as well as an authentic and difficult test of truth, all the more justified since "only the truth sets us free."

As in any other field of research, psychoanalysis elaborates working hypotheses, many of which prove to be, in practice, extremely helpful. There is a level of lower functioning, unconscious and mechanical, where we are indisputably conditioned by factors that psychoanalysis has very clearly defined. Furthermore, it introduces, in terms of energy, a dynamic (in the sense of conflicting forces) approach to psychic processes; and this, to me, is the most interesting aspect of the revolution of ideas that it represents.

I should mention, however, that highly developed conceptions of the transformation of energy, especially of sexual energy, have always existed in traditional teachings, such as Tantrism—to mention only this one. Freud, in contradistinction to Jung, was not favorably disposed to making a real study of them. It seems to me his system does not open to transcendence.

Doubtless it is difficult, when one steps into a system, to see anything except what the system shows you, to avoid its specific blindness. But it is possible, in my opinion, without falling into syncretism, to carry on work of a psychoanalytical nature without adhering to the general doctrine. It is possible to center the work—as, moreover, Freud insisted toward the end—not on interpretation, but primarily on awareness in depth of resistances and on objectifying them, in order to help the ego free itself within its essential function, that of lucidity. It remains for it then to assume its role before many great mysteries, which place guilt in another perspective as a stimulating factor for larger and higher responsibility. And this responsible choice cannot be reduced to a sort of obligatory, civilized retreat into sublimation; it arises from listening to the echo within ourselves of a definite call to be.

P. From this more conscious level, are there steps that might be taken to enable the ego to accept or refuse the judgment of the super-ego, and thus escape from unconscious guilt?

M. de S. Well, of course, first of all we should use our ability to test reality—our ability not to confuse what we actually perceive with what we represent to ourselves. In observing our life more closely, we must certainly be struck by how far from objective we are and how much we interpret and react according to our fantasies, emotional reactions, or conditioning.

This, by the way, shows the importance of sound education. We should not only teach principles but let them be practically tested and experienced. Guilt is closely related to ignorance of what reality is. Let us not forget that law transgression, for instance, may have beneficial aspects: it awakens us to a better understanding of a real order. The original meaning of "carnival" was the intentional, temporary turning upside-down of every-thing, the throwing out of all values, in order to refresh and clarify the inward and outward need for order. Of course, there must be proper indications for such a medicine; in an orderless life, "carnival" just brings more disorder.

The law reminds us that guilt is inseparable from responsibility—that is, from the existence of an alternative, of a choice. We are thus led to the problem of free will, of freedom. But none of this would exist without consciousness. One might say that consciousness is the key to freedom— freedom to see the choice, to start with. But this key is much more rarely used than we think. Most of the time there is no real consciousness of what takes place in us. We take for consciousness what really is simply perception, instead of the result of a confrontation of our situation with all that constitutes our make-up. Most of the time we follow what we passively call "the better choice," essentially in order not to be misjudged by others. We have inherited a system of values with which we identify ourselves, but I think we should try to make use of it more actively, try somehow to deserve it, see whether we can really make it ours and not simply remain slaves of it. In other words, I think it is important to develop clearly an idea, an ego-ideal which is felt as independent from the super-ego. This ideal might be lucidity.

P. You touch here something very important, that in our times it seems essential to clarify. In some people, especially those of older generations, the betrayal of their super-ego immediately engenders guilt feelings. In other people there is no guilt, not even that of a delinquent; there is instead a sort of notion of natural freedom without constraint. This ideal is obviously reflected in today's society where authority is flouted and values are overthrown. One attempts to turn towards an ideal distant from the super-ego but it nevertheless remains marked by it; it is a way of escape from conformist guilt, but one is recaptured by another form of recognized opinion, which is not lucidity.

M. de s. I quite agree. Lucidity is a very high objective. One must first become aware of all the pulls to which the ego is submitted—we have talked about that—and then of the various unconscious defense mechanisms which it has elaborated to protect itself against what it does not want to see. This is particularly difficult to grasp. Other obstacles are raised by the power of suggestion, the tendencies inherent in our character, our various habits, the mechanisms of projection and identification, etc. A great inner tranquility is needed to estimate, understand, taste in a direct, experiential way the instability of the ego. Psychoanalytical experience helps toward that, and so do relaxation techniques when well oriented.

It is a progressive work, going through stages. Trying to succeed immediately in obtaining results is an additional obstacle. As one goes one, one learns to keep in touch with difficulties, to see them in order to get free from them.

In fact, the ego is our attention. It needs to be free and pure. Only through our errors, our gropings, the many traps that threaten our attention, can we discover the way to interiority. All authentic spiritual ways lead to that. But the way is very long. To become conformable to one's essential nature is the most anti-conformist work that can be conceived. It needs total freedom of attention. Meditation and a wide range of exercises are necessary. But fortunately, through what in Christianity is called "grace," light is given, orientation comes, a call is heard. Doubtless, it needs a great quietness, emptiness, transparency to let this influence work upon us. But it is far from being a passive state; it is an action that requires ultimate awareness from the whole being.

P. You have spoken of grace. It is a word which does not suggest any image, any form, any structure.

M. de s. Yes; and analogically, pure attention is beyond word, form, image, and thought—I mean our usual thought. It is often referred to as a living light. When it acts, duality merges into oneness. There is no more room for guilt then. Guilt—or to use a better word, conscious remorse—is nevertheless of dynamic help to put ourselves into question, and recall us to the need of being present, of being purely attentive.

P. Could we say that the idea of guilt could become indeed a very healthy and powerful catalyst, if we didn't stick to its usual superficial image? If it is taken as a real mystery that has to be explored, like the idea that it originates with the fall of man; if we accept it as a provocation to live a mystery, a research, then this confused feeling becomes a dynamic support in the search for lucidity, especially if we accept not to succeed and continue constantly to re-explore the mystery. The great danger is to accept that without questioning it; it would then lose its power.

M. de S. Yes; but we must admit there are degrees, levels, in any learning process. The mystery issues into the infinite, which by definition cannot be defined. But guilt at first refers to idols, to objects of the mind; and spiritual evolution may involve passing from one idol to another until you are able to live the mystery fully. You necessarily start in duality until you reach a point where there is no observer and no observed. Idol dependency is, I think, related to our dependency upon the big world of associations. All our psychic life is governed by the associative process, of which we may nevertheless become conscious. It is terribly difficult to escape this dense dynamic network, but still it is possible to become free from it, thanks to other laws operating in watchfulness.

P. Among intellectuals and scientists, the acceptance of idols of course raises guilt feelings—as if they were afraid of regressing to some barbarian state and want to make a stand against everything that could appear spiritual.

M. de S. I quite share this resistance towards whatever is believed without experimenting and experiencing. Science may be an idol as well. For me, real spirituality is as rigorous as science. They should not contradict but complement each other in order to find what is beyond and animates them both. This attitude seems to gain more and more ground among researchers. André Malraux, one of our great writers, who under de Gaulle's government was appointed a minister of culture, even ventured, these prophetic words: "The twenty-first century will be religious or it will not be at all!"

P. Would you think there is more guilt in individuals and in society now than in our parents' or grandparents' time?

M. de S. Yes, at first sight it seems paradoxical—probably because of our rooted belief in the idea of evolution and progress, and because there has indeed been amazing progress made from many points of view—but I would nevertheless say there is more guilt today.

As concerns individuals, many observations can be made. There is for instance evident liberalization of sex since the fifties, but it does not necessarily mean that emotional maturity has followed it. We know that "acting out" is not at all a liberation from repression, and the increase—observed in the medical milieu—of male impotence among young people, of frigidity, of sexual perversions and homosexuality, certainly pleads in favor of unresolved guilt problems.

We also feel powerless in the face of all the problems on a planetary scale with which we are now confronted daily by the media. Sociological and ecological dangers, as well as technology's threats of destruction, mobilize anxiety and our latent guilt feelings all the more because we do not see clearly what can be done, and what is being done doesn't make us feel more secure. I imagine the dreams of present state leaders would be informative with respect to your question. As never before, both the individual and society are confronted with the inescapable necessity to call forth all their potentials to solve the world's vital, overwhelming problems.

We are going through a crisis of civilization where older values are severely shaken and new values not yet settled. We are not supported any more by a system of clearly accepted principles, giving meaning to all aspects and events of our daily life. In our modern society life has been progressively deritualized, desacralized. Such institutions as marriage, family, state, etc., have lost their structuring function. Pragmatic and economic points of view have discarded the old holistic conceptions of the world. And man is not an animal; his make-up is such that meaning is of higher importance to him than food or sex. Totally deprived of meaning, he falls into guilt or depression. This essential need for meaning, which rationalism does not answer satisfactorily, is reflected, I think, in the present blossoming of new religions and sects.

Lack of true meaning, that is, of sound relation to what exists around us, makes us feel lonely and ego-centered. Egoism and separateness are, I think, deep motives for guilt.

15

◆

An Interview with
Seyyed Hossein Nasr

"Wholeness," VOL. X:1, February, 1985

The Long Journey

No scholar has contributed more than Dr. Seyyed Hossein Nasr to the restoration, in recent years, of tradition and the traditional sciences to their rightful place as authentic branches of human knowledge. His lectures, essays, and authoritative books on Islamic science and metaphysics have alerted many to the rich possibilities of this perspective.

Born in Teheran in 1933, Dr. Nasr studied mathematics and physics at M.I.T. before receiving his doctorate in the history of science and philosophy from Harvard University in 1958. For twenty-one years, he was a professor of Islamic philosophy and the history of science at Teheran University. In 1974, Dr. Nasr founded and served as the first president of the Iranian Academy of Philosophy, a position he held until 1979. In 1981, he became the first Muslim invited to deliver the prestigious Gifford Lectures at the University of Edinburgh. He is at present University Professor of Islamic Studies at The George Washington University in Washington, D.C.

♦

PARABOLA In your essay "Sufism and the Integration of Man," which appears in your book *Sufi Essays*, you write that "Islam is the religion of unity. . . . " and that " . . . the whole programme of Sufism . . . is to free man from the prison of multiplicity, to cure him from hypocrisy, and to make him whole, for it is only in being whole that man can become holy." How would you define the whole man? What are his attributes?

SEYYED HOSSEIN NASR The whole man is a person who realizes fully what it means to be man. That is, he has, or she has—and throughout this essay when I say "man" I mean both sexes—within himself realized all the possibilities of existence, the perfection of all the qualities with which God—ultimate Reality—has embellished human nature, but which is not fully manifested in all members of the human race. This idea goes back, of course, to the central Sufi doctrine of the Perfect Man or the Universal Man, *al-Insan al-kamil,* according to which every creature reflects in its own way some aspect, or quality, of the Divine Nature, some Divine Name or Divine Quality in its specific Islamic reference. (*al-Asma' wa'l-Sifat.*) Only man is the mirror of all the Divine Names and Qualities. Therefore, to say "Man" is to say "totality" and "wholeness": that is, all aspects of the Supreme Divinity which have manifested themselves in the cosmos. Now, to be whole is to realize this fullness of our own nature. The Sufi answer to your question would be very simple: in order for a man to be whole, all he or she has to do is to be himself or herself; that is, to realize what we really are in our ultimate reality, which is to be the total reflection, total image, total theophany of God's Names and Qualities.

P. How do we realize what we really are? I may have an idea about wholeness, about the perfect man, but I see *myself* fragmented. How does one become whole?

S.H.N. The very fact that we pose such a question means that there exists within our mind and soul an echo, no matter how faint, and a light, no matter how dim, of that wholeness. Why is it that we who are fragmented even talk about wholeness? It means we have a reminiscence in our being of being whole. Now here lies in fact the key to your question: namely, wholeness brings with it the certitude of its own reality, precisely because the human being is composed of multiple levels of existence, of different powers—physical, mental, psychological, spiritual; and this is very important, not to mistake the spiritual for the psychological, or the mental for the intellectual, which is the other aspect of the spiritual. Because man possesses all of these faculties inwardly, unless he gains access to them there is always a sense of loss.

It's as if you asked me the question, "How do I know when water quenches my thirst?" If you get hold of real water and have real thirst, the very drinking of the water will quench your thirst, and nothing else. There is within the nature of man a quest for wholeness, which is itself a great miracle because we are not whole. Where do we get this urge? Where did we find the origin of the idea of wholeness? Deep down within ourselves, that wholeness from which we have become separated by our externalized existence beckons us. It calls upon us. And the call continues until we hearken to its voice and are able to live in such a way as to fulfill the innate need for wholeness; and questions as to how we reach it are really theoretical. The thirst we have to externalize ourselves—the need for satisfaction through an action which is external to ourselves and therefore which is against what wholeness really implies—continues in us. We all have it; it is the root of all our miseries. But it is never fulfilled unless it turns upon itself, moves in an inward direction—rather than outward—and reaches wholeness. Unless a person reaches wholeness, that craving never ceases. Its goal may change, but the fire is never extinguished except through the proximity of the Sacred which wholeness implies.

P. Is it possible for an ordinary person leading an ordinary life in an honorable and just way to achieve wholeness, or is special guidance necessary? Is a teacher necessary?

S.H.N. If we could only break the ice which separates our everyday awareness of ourselves from the spring of eternal life which resides at our heart, in the center of our being, we would neither need a teacher nor a revelation. But man, that is, man in the present cycle of humanity—at the time of Adam all men were prophets—man in this day and age cannot break that ice without the help of God—without the help of the ultimate source of our own being—and without the help of a teacher. Wholeness on the highest level belongs only to a great saint in the sense that everything that person does always comes from a single center: and that is why only a saint is beyond hypocrisy. But that highest level of wholeness is not achievable for everyone. There are lower levels, however; there's a kind of hierarchy of wholeness. On a more restricted level there are the teachings of religion, which are meant for everyone; for example, the Divine Law in Islam, the *Shari'ah*, if practiced faithfully, produces a degree of wholeness and integration in life which is sufficient for a man to live happily and to die in felicity, but not sufficient to realize wholeness on the highest level, which is union with the Divine and all that implies: the integration of all aspects of our being and the awareness of the One at the highest level. For that stage to be attained there's always need of a teacher, and if there are exceptions, it is only to prove the rule.

I always come back to the beautiful saying of the Gospels, when Christ mentions, "The wind bloweth where it listeth." I learned the significance of this many, many years ago from a writing of Frithjof Schuon, where he spoke about the possibility of the Spirit manifesting itself where God wills, outside the ways in which we would expect. And this saying has many applications, one of which is the answer to your question: that it is possible for certain exceptional individuals to be pulled by the attraction of Heaven without a human teacher. But that possibility, although it might be realized in certain cases, is not an excuse for not having a spiritual teacher, nor does it manifest itself very often. So one comes back to the famous saying of Bayazid, the great Sufi of Khorasan, who said that the spiritual master of those who have no spiritual master is the Devil. This integration of the higher faculties of the soul, which surely belong to God, is impossible without the help of a person who has already undergone the process of this integration, because one otherwise deals with very powerful and dangerous forces which often, under the guise of integration, lead to disintegration and permanent damage to an aspect of the soul which really only God and the Sacred can mold and remold.

P. Is it possible for those who are not following a particular religious path to achieve any degree of wholeness?

S.H.N. If I can emphasize "any degree," then yes. There are people, especially in this day and age in which many, because of the loss of the more metaphysical dimensions of the Western religions, have fallen out of their traditions and are looking for something, who may live close to nature and its beauties; and having a kind of simple soul which is satisfied with the grace emanating from the natural environment, they may attain through that a certain degree of wholeness. But man is not just a "natural" being in that sense. Such people carry within themselves, of course, those deeper layers of the soul, and the problem of not having integrated those elements into the conscious aspect of their being manifests itself sooner or later. To integrate those elements, one has to live according to one of the traditions, one of the religions which God has revealed. I do not believe that wholeness, in the higher levels of the meaning of this word, and as it gradually becomes synonymous with holiness, is possible without the door having opened from the heavenly side towards humanity. Man cannot force this door open by himself, and the door always opens from the divine side. You might say it is the Logos that descends—that Avatar that descends from Heaven—who then opens up the path which we then follow from this side.

P. What are the chief obstacles that a man will face on the path towards wholeness? What is it in ourselves that keeps us from wholeness?

S.H.N. Christianity would say that it is original sin; Islam does not believe in original sin, but believes that the chief impediment is forgetfulness. But I want to answer this in a kind of present-day, "existential" manner, as it concerns the predicament of modern man. If you'd asked this question of me a hundred years ago, when my ancestors lived in Kashan—if God had willed that I'd be teaching there then, rather than a hundred years later, here in Washington—I would have answered that the chief impediment, of course, is this veil of forgetfulness which covers our inner nature. This veil has to do with our passions, with what the Koran calls *al-nafs al-ammarah*; that is, the part of our soul which commands us to do evil—the passionate, externalizing, dissipating aspect of our soul. That would be the major obstacle.

Today, however, there's another very major obstacle which the men of old did not face. Then, human beings—in normal situations, at least—knew that there was such as thing as wholeness. Today men face first of all the obstacle of not even being clear as to the existence of wholeness, to say nothing of its attainment. If you were a Muslim, or a Christian, or a Hindu, living traditionally, you would not ask yourself the question, "Is there such a thing as wholeness, and is there a path towards it?" You would ask yourself the question, "Do I want to follow this path or not?" You knew that a path was there; for instance, if you were in the Islamic world, you knew that the Khangah or Zawiyah, the Sufi center, was there, that there were people who followed the path of wholeness. Today the first obstacle is that many human beings are forced to ask, for the first time in the history of the world as we know it, "What is the meaning of life, anyway?"; that is, having to discover the questions of certitude and doubt, of truth and falsehood, by themselves. And therefore the first obstacle is precisely to remove our ignorance of the nature of Reality, if I can express it in an intellectual language; or, in a religious manner, to discover the goal of life: that it is in fact possible to be whole, and therefore it is a desirable goal. And once decided which goal to follow, whom should I choose as master? Now there is a choice which did not even present itself to any humanity before us, and that is the possibility of even choosing one's religion. Except in rare situations, such as in Kashmir in the thirteenth century, this was never a choice to be made by human beings.

There is of course also a great compensation in all of this, in that since this first obstacle presents an exceptional challenge, once it's overcome God makes the second obstacle much more easy to surmount. A traditional Muslim, Hindu, Jew, or Buddhist accepted with certitude the truth of their religion. In the traditional situation the skeptic was not one who doubted God or his tradition, but who within that world of certitude might be skeptical about certain schools, certain trends of thought. And therefore to follow the spiritual path, to be placed under the direct beam of the Divine Grace which shines upon us, was a much more difficult feat to achieve. Today attraction of Divine Grace is made easier by the very difficulty of our predicament, the difficulty of the human situation. And for that reason, although the obstacles have changed, perhaps because of God's justice, the attainment is not that much more difficult. It's just the type of difficulty which is altered with present-day humanity.

P. The first obstacle you speak of, the difficulty of people today to begin focusing on their internal situation, is a serious one. There are fewer and fewer nations where true spiritual teaching is available. Why is this? Is this a consequence of an internal flaw in religions themselves, that people are less and less interested in their teachings?

S.H.N. This is again a question which can be answered in two different ways. From one point of view one could say that the inner meaning of religions becomes less and less accessible, to the extent that human beings become less qualified to understand that inner meaning. Secondly, in fact present-day humanity doesn't deserve anything more than it is able to attain. That is, it is the externalization of man today which makes the inward less accessible. But having said that, I want to add that in fact the inner dimension is not completely inaccessible. There is again a kind of divine compensation, putting aside all the pseudo-teachers and pseudo-gurus who provide a kind of spiritual guidance in reverse, from below rather than from above, and whose teachings correspond in effect to the subversion of so much of what remains of religion in the modern world. Putting that phenomenon aside, I would say that, first of all, authentic spiritual instruction can never cease completely without the world collapsing. There's a saying in Arabic according to which the earth shall never become empty of the person who's witness to God, who is a true spiritual teacher. That cannot happen; that's not metaphysically possible.

And at a more externalized level, precisely because you have this eclipse of the normal methods of attaining spiritual instruction, there is a kind of casting of the inward outward by the authorities of tradition, in the highest sense of the word: an externalization which has never been available before. Before this day and age you never had a humanity which could read the greatest pearls of wisdom of all the religions just by going into any bookstore, like the Yes! bookshop three blocks from here, and being able to read Lao Tzu and the Upanishads and Sufi masterpieces and Meister Eckhart and Hasidic writings and the Kabbala and God knows what. What does this phenomenon mean? Why is it that the most gifted spiritual person in even a country like India, or Persia, which have been great centers of mysticism in days gone by, did not have such a possibility? It means that you have again, because of this compensation which exists in the Divine and the human order, a kind of availability of things which in themselves were difficult of access before. Look at Judaism: if you were living in Spain in the fourteenth and fifteen centuries, you would have belonged to a Jewish community which represented one of the peaks of Jewish culture. And at that time there were masters of Lurian Kabbala. What would you have had to do in order to be able to read some of these texts? After perhaps twenty years of studying Hebrew with this teacher and that teacher, finally you might be taught Lurian Kabbala. And now any kid as a college freshman can go and pick up the Zohar or the books of Lurian Kabbala in a bookstore.

This is not equal to instruction, of course, but even the theoretical exposition of that type of doctrine in the modern world has something to do with the question you posed, and this instruction has not become completely unavailable. To the extent that humanity falls spiritually and becomes more and more externalized, less and less interested in the inner dimensions of religion, these dimensions recede, without dying out completely. Those inner dimensions have receded most for that humanity which has externalized itself most: Europe and Western civilization. And to the extent that Islam, Hinduism, Buddhism, or Oriental Judaism undergo the same process, the inner dimension of the religion becomes less and less accessible. But by means of the compensation of which I've spoken, the door always remains open; and that is because ultimately we are responsible before God, and God is just. For the person who seeks, the saying of Christ, "Seek and ye shall find," will hold true until He returns. That was not a temporal statement. But where you have to knock, and where you will find, may be different from days gone by.

P. Assuming one begins to walk towards the open door of which you speak, one examines oneself and sees one's fragmentary nature. You spoke earlier about the passions. What is a useful attitude towards our fragmented nature, towards our passions? Should we eradicate them, or use them? How does remembrance, of which you also spoke, enter in here?

S.H.N. I'm always very careful when questions like this are asked of me. Spiritual instruction is not meant for general public consumption. Religions, in their exoteric form and with their general instructions, are. Commandments such as: you should be good, you should not lie, you should be humble, and the Ten Commandments: these are for all men. But how to control the passions? What to do with them? The alchemy of the transformation of human passions is not exactly the same for all human beings. So I am opposed to giving a generalized answer to these questions, except as it concerns general principles. The case of each aspirant is different.

But in a general sense, there is a stage in the spiritual life when one has to slay the dragon—not the Chinese dragon, which in Chinese alchemy means the power of the soul as it grows wings and flies, but dragon in the sense of a sort of fiendish demonic force which prevents the hero from reaching the treasure, as in our children's stories in Western Europe and Asia as well as in America. This dragon has to be slain by the spiritual power which St. George and St. Michael represent; and their lance represents a direct Divine Presence without which it is not possible to slay this dragon. The dragon is *much* more powerful than we are. We are swallowed up very easily. That's why we can read a book about all these things and feel that we have mastered the subject; we may be very disciplined for fifteen or twenty minutes or even longer, but then the first wind that blows topples us over, because we have not as yet slain the dragon. It is therefore necessary that, at the beginning of the path, you be able to slay the dragon, to subdue this passion. The Sufis refer to this principle by saying that we have to make the devil in us Muslim; that is, make the rebellious nature in us surrender itself to God.

Now, this process implies a kind of death. When we say "life," what do we mean by it? We mean this everyday consciousness, which is really the forgetfulness of God. We remember our everyday ambitions—to eat, to enjoy ourselves in the evening, to get up in the morning; we remember everything except the one thing that Christ said you should remember, the one thing necessary. And therefore to kill this consciousness is really "to die." So the first stage is a death, a purgation. That is universal in all spiritual paths. But that death does not kill our immortal soul; it leads to its coming to life. So the next stage is the stage of expansion, of the coming to life of the inner aspects which had been hidden by the force of this dragon which was suffocating them. And that in turn leads to union, to the fruit of the path, which is knowledge of God and love of God. So I would say that the three universal stages of contraction, expansion, and union, as Evelyn Underhill mentions, pertain in one way or another to all spiritual paths.

P. In "Sufism and the Integration of Man" you mention Rūmī writing that the adept in the spiritual retreat must invoke the Holy Name until his toes begin to say "Allah." What is the role of the body in the search for wholeness?

S.H.N. In Islam, as in the other two monotheistic religions, wholeness includes the body. Why is it that all three religions believe in the resurrection of the body on the Day of Judgment? When we stand before God, in that final moment of encounter which determines the whole destiny of human beings—all of this life is a journey towards that one moment, of encounter with God—our body, according to those theologies, is present along with our soul. Take the Christian case: Christ ascended to heaven bodily. The Catholics believe that the Virgin Mary also ascended to heaven corporeally. Judaism has the chariot of Elias. Islam has the ascension of the Prophet, *al-mi'rāj*, which was a corporeal ascent, not just a spiritual one, the latter being open to everyone—*al-mi'rāj al-ruham*. So the body is somehow part of that whole of which we are speaking.

What Sufism tries to do is to disassociate the soul from excessive attention to the bodily passions, while the body remains, in a sense, neutral. The body is in fact from another point of view very positive, because it is created by God and doesn't have the independence which our soul has to rebel against God. Say you have an atheist who says, "I don't believe in God." His pulse continues to beat, however, and his liver continues to function. And that organic functioning is seen from the Islamic point of view as meaning that these organs are following God's command, irrespective of the conscious mind which might deny God or His Will.

Now, in the second, later stage of the path, as the soul becomes purified it does not leave the body—the body is still there, we're still alive—and it realizes the significance of the body as God's creation and as a temple of the spirit. The idea of the body as a temple is very, very important, for it is related to the great influence and effect that a transmuted sensuality, which is also spiritual, has upon the spiritual life. Man is the bridge between heaven and earth. On the one hand, he is to leave earth for heaven; on the other, he is to bring back heaven on earth. He is to serve as a conduit, a channel, for Divine Grace, *barakah*. And this sensualized spirituality—which is so important in Sufism and which often is manifested in the forms of eroticism, and the love for perfume, and for beauty—has to do with the positive function that the body then plays in this very important duty of the spiritualized man to transmit the Divine Presence to the world about him, including the world of nature.

At the same time, the body represents the outer limits of our individuality, and therefore when it participates in the divine rites we are sure that we are participating wholly in them. That's why Jalāl a-Dīn Rūmī says that you should sit down and invoke the name of God until your toes say "Allah, Allah"; this incredible poem in the *Mathnawi* refers to the very esoteric and of course never publicly divulged practices according to which, finally, the body participates in the prayer of the heart, and man realizes the function of the body as an extension of the heart, of our inner center, and therefore an *extremely* important container of what we call the soul. If we will only remain in our bodies we would become perfect masters of meditation; because the one thing in us which never stays put is our mind. And the body can play an important role in the actual process of bridling the mind. If we could only live our mental life within the body we would become masters of the contemplative path. All one has to do is to place oneself in God's Name and place the Name in the heart. But how hard it is to achieve this apparently simple action.

P. It has been said, "Be aware of every breath."

S.H.N. Yes, that of course is an allusion to the spiritual technique of the invocation of the Name of God, which in fact has to do with the expansion of the breast, since the lungs exist within the breast, and each breath expands the lungs. Breathing is not only related to the fundamental pulse which enables human life to continue, it also is the rhythm which, in the Sufi who's aware of the presence of God, relates him to God. So every time you breathe and you don't remember God, in a sense you've failed to achieve wholeness, and have fallen below the perfection of wholeness.

P. In the search for wholeness, do men and women have different paths to travel? Or is the path the same for both?

S.H.N. First of all, the male and female natures are not accidental. The differences are not only biological, and not only psychological. The differences do not stop even on the spiritual level, but have their roots in the Divine Nature itself. The principles of male and female represent essentially a complementarity which goes back to God Himself. All this debate now about God as Himself or as Herself is due to the forgetting of the metaphysical doctrine of the Divine Nature which always embraces both aspects or poles. God in His Essence—or Its Essence—is above all duality; at the same time, God's Infinitude is the principle of femininity *in divinis*, while God's Absoluteness is the principle or Divine Prototype of masculinity. At the root of what appears on the human plane as the male and female stands the Divine Nature, and there is nothing accidental about the male-female distinction. There is such a thing as female spirituality. There is such a thing as male spirituality. Of course, all human beings also contain both of these elements within themselves to some degree.

As far as the practices of Sufism are concerned, they are the same for men and women. Both are seen as immortal beings with the possibility of reaching the Divine. And that is because men and women complement each other and reflect their common androgynic origin. They're both whole and segmented. That is why the possibilities of both celibacy and sexual union have spiritual significance: because both realities are present in human nature. A person who lives a celibate life wants to show that he or she is, in fact, an image of the whole without the need of the other sex; that is the basis of celibacy in Buddhism and in Christianity. Whereas in the other philosophy, as it exists in Islam and Judaism and Hinduism, in which sexuality is positive and in which one encounters a powerful current of spiritualized sexuality, it is sexual union which symbolizes the complementarity of the male and the female, and hence wholeness. So both of these possibilities are realizable and have to be contained in any major spiritual path. All of the injunctions of the *Shari'ah* are the same for men and women; all the fasting, the daily prayers, the paying of alms, the going on pilgrimage, the responsibility for moral action, the question of the judgment of God—except during the menstrual period of a woman, when she does not perform her daily prayers and does not fast—the general instructions and practices are the same. But the nuances, the delicacies of what spiritual instruction is given to a particular individual, are not the same. They are not something to be promulgated in a general manner for everyone whether man or woman. It's like what I said before about the differences between individuals. Every serious Sufi master takes into consideration the differences between his or her male and female disciples as well as between members of each sex. It needs to be mentioned that there are also women spiritual masters in Sufism; not just disciples. Perhaps the number has been less but there have been some very great women spiritual masters and saints. So while there is no black-and-white difference of spiritual techniques for men and women in Sufism, at the same time male and female spirituality are recognized for what they are, and that in some way, in every human being who's of a spiritual nature, these elements are intertwined.

P. You speak of every human being who's of a spiritual nature. Why are some people called to seek a spiritual way, and others not?

S.H.N. There are many esoteric teachings, especially in Islam, which allude to the fact that we had some kind of reality before we were born with a certain nature that defines us. The moment of history in which we entered the temporal cycle, where we were born, and with what powers and possibilities, are all related to the state that we had before we came into what we call the terrestrial life. It is very difficult—in fact, impossible from the point of human intelligence—to give the exact reasons why you were born in New York, I was born in Teheran, a third person in Belgium; why you and I were born in the twentieth century; someone else in the thirteenth century; why you may be a very good musician, and I a very bad one; or, why a particular person has a deep love for God and some other person doesn't. It seems that the moment we enter into the terrestrial life, what we bring to this world already depends on who we are. Astrology tries to deal with this a bit, relating it to the progression of the stars. But it needs much more than astrological knowledge to be able to relate what one is and the situation of one's life. Of course, heredity has a lot to do with it. But the question remains, "Why is it that we are born of a particular father and mother?" These questions are not easy to answer in context of our discussion because they need a great deal of metaphysical preparation. Not all human beings start from the same point either intellectually or spiritually. But because we are human, because we all have the imprint of the Divine upon our forehead, God's justice requires that we all have the same access to Him. And that is why religion in its general formulation never excludes any of its followers.

But the inner teachings of a religion have to be for those who are prepared to receive them. If all human beings had the same yearning or love for God, then the inner teachings would be for everyone; but this is not the case of human reality. And no religion can fail to cater to the needs of the few who seek God here and now—because it always is those few who seek God who are like the salt of society. The religion which cannot cater to the needs of its potential saints and sages gradually ceases to have saints, and then fissures begin to appear in its walls, leading to its collapse. The exoteric body of the religion begins to decompose. Therefore the need for the inner teaching reserved for the few is present because of the different capabilities of human beings. It seems that human beings stand in different points on this long journey of man from God and to God. We are all equal in that we shall stand before Him on the Day of Judgment and will be judged accordingly—His laws are for all of us—but how close we are to Him now and what knowledge of Him we have now and our love for

Him now—those are not equal.

P. Does a person who's achieved wholeness, or a great degree of wholeness, have a particular role to play towards his or her fellow humanity?

S.H.N. What is really forgotten is that it is the human being's vocation which determines what he should do—what the Buddhists call his *dharma*. We must follow our own nature. There are those whom God has willed that after gaining wholeness they should do things for other human beings. There are others whom God has willed simply to be, which is a very, very important manner of serving mankind. Like the light above our heads: it doesn't *do* anything, but it illuminates this whole room. It is this function of wholeness which has been belittled in the modern world, to the great detriment of the modern world, with its over-emphasis on action. And there are other human beings whose vocation is to *make*; that is, people who are artistic.

So I do not want to give a single answer. There are three different modes of reflecting wholeness. One is through service, charity on all levels; for example, Christian saints who created hospitals for the poor—and that must not be mixed up with that kind of atheistic charity in the modern world which wants to be good despite God. I'm speaking of traditionally religious charity and living a life of service, like the Karma yoga of the Hindus. A person who is whole lives this life in a manner that is whole, and there's tremendous effect in the actions which such a person performs. That's something which many people forget: the quality of the action of a person who is whole differs from the quality of others' actions. What he says, the way he looks at people: the deep effect that is left is due to the fact that it comes from a different source of action, a different layer of inner being.

The second mode of making, the whole field of *ars*—not art in the modern sense, but the Latin *ars*. Such a person might be simply a gardener, or the holder of some small job; it doesn't need to be grandiose in the modern Western sense. A person with wholeness would bring this quality to whatever he would make or do. All his activity would be "art." In traditional civilization, a gardener or a woodcutter could be a man who had a great deal of wholeness, and whatever he did would reflect this wholeness in a manner which benefited those around him.

And the third is what is called the mode of being, that of those whose whole function it is to either disseminate knowledge—whose act of charity it is to teach—or to simply be a presence, not "to do anything" but simply to be a sort of silent witness to God. They're like a window onto the world of light.

There is no rivalry between these various modes, and it's a great tragedy that there has been polemical writing during the last century over this issue, with people attacking even the great medieval saints, because they did not cater to the needs of the poor. This modern aberration is due to a total misunderstanding of the nature of the world of man and of God. It has led to this terrible situation today when much of theology is destroyed in the name of human service, without human service in fact getting any better despite this sacrilegious sacrifice as a result of which the functions of theology have become nearly forgotten.

P. Do you have any practical advice for someone who's beginning to sense the need for more wholeness in his or her life?

S.H.N. The person who already feels a lack of wholeness has received a gift from heaven. We say in Sufism that the only person whose ignorance is incurable is a person who doesn't know that he is ignorant. To know that one is ignorant is already the first stage of cure from ignorance. In the same way, to realize that one is lacking wholeness is already a blessing from heaven. The important thing is, to be true to one's self; never to relent in one's quest for wholeness. The great danger is a kind of momentary and passing state which appears as equilibrium or a small degree of wholeness, and which leads to forgetting that this was just a step or a station house on the path, not the goal. The quest for wholeness, which enters into the heart of a person, should never come to an end unless one really gains wholeness in the ultimate sense. One must find the way which suits one's nature and for which one is made. Once this occurs, it is the path which will decide for us. But of course from an inner point of view it's always the path that chooses the man, and not the man who chooses the path.

16

◆

An Interview with
His Holiness the Dalai Lama
by Robert A.F. Thurman

"Wholeness," VOL. X:1, February, 1985

The Fullness of Emptiness

$H$is Holiness Tenzin Gyatso, the 14th Dalai Lama of *Tibet, has a number of principal identities. He is a Buddhist monk in the Order founded by Shakyamuni Buddha around 525 B.C.E. and revitalized by Lama Tson Khapa around 1400; hence, a spokesman for the ancient educational tradition of the Buddhists. He is a reincarnation of the Buddha Avalokateshvara, the Mahayana Buddhist Archangel of Compassion, and especially the Savior of Tibetans, the King of Tibet (tragically in exile for the last twenty-five years); hence, the defender of rights and freedoms of Tibetans. And he is a Vajra Master of the esoteric Mandalas of the Unexcelled Yoga Tantras, especially of the Kalachakra Wheel of Time; hence deeply and perhaps prophetically concerned with the positive evolution of all intelligent life in our sacred environment on this planet.*

Dr. Thurman is a professor of Religion at Amherst College, a founder of the American Institute of Buddhist Studies, and an old friend and student of His Holiness's since 1964. This interview was conducted at the Deanery at Westminster Abbey, where His Holiness was staying as the guest of the Very Reverend Dean and Mrs. Carpenter, in the mixture of Tibetan and English His Holiness and Professor Thurman tend to speak when they discuss the Dharma in terms of its relevance to today. Dr. Thurman presented His Holiness with a number of questions suggested by PARABOLA.

ROBERT THURMAN Your Holiness, PARABOLA Magazine would like to ask you about "Wholeness"—the Whole Man, the Whole Person. They say: "We are defining the Whole Person as one who has in his being, to a very high degree, freedom, unity, consciousness, and will. What is your view?"

HIS HOLINESS What I call the human qualities are love, compassion, tolerance, will. To be warm-hearted—that is true human being. You see, not to have warm feeling in the heart, that is almost not to have fully the nature of a human.

R.T. Would you say, finally, that Buddha is Whole Man?

H.H. Yes—on a high level. Yes, certainly. But when I speak of the good qualities of a human being, that means our ordinary human being, on the human level. Buddha is already beyond the human level.

R.T. If Buddha is beyond ordinary human nature, then some people might think of him as cold-hearted—someone sort of superhuman, that doesn't care.

H.H. No, no, no, no. What we call Buddha is warm-heartedness developed infinitely, love perfected. And also infinite enlightened consciousness—oh, yes.

R.T. Their next question is: "It has been said that the Whole Person is one who lives simultaneously in two worlds. Do you agree with this, and if so, what does it mean to you?"

H.H. This has different meanings. One: the person himself or herself reaches the highest level, but meantime, remains in world affairs—for the sake of other beings, out of altruism. In that way, "living in two worlds" can be said. Then again, maybe another meaning: a person who really practices well, and as a result, for himself or herself there is no sort of emotion, but equanimity. One is impartial; but in accordance with circumstances, taking certain action. In his inner world, there are no differences, but in his outer world he or she keeps aware of differences, and accordingly takes action. So you see, two worlds, I think, can be understood on different levels.

R.T. "Is there a fully realized, totally developed whole within every human being? Or does the process of struggling to free oneself of ignorance contribute to the perfecting of the individual? In other words, is there only a seed of a liberated being within, which must grow through effort?"

H.H. I think this is correct. In other words, what we call the Buddha-nature—that is the Buddha seed. That means of course there are different aspects of Buddha nature. One aspect is *shūnya**: "the reality of the mind which needs not to abandon any taints." That is what we call Buddha nature, according to the *Ornament of Realizations*. Also, *Sugatagarbha*: according to the *Supreme Tantra*, that also is Buddha nature, and the ultimate nature of consciousness is also called Buddha nature: *Tathāgatagarbha*. So you see, from that viewpoint, the seed of liberated being comes right from the beginning; that seed is there. But that is not sufficient. Just by being there, there's no benefit, right? So you see, one needs effort, to develop, to purify oneself, on the basis of that nature.

R.T. Is it that the fact of that seed being there makes it possible to do it? Without it. . . .

H.H. Without it that can't happen. There is no sense in purifying a stone, even though it has the nature of emptiness also. But because the other aspects of the Buddha nature are not there, we can't say that the stone ultimately becomes Buddha.

R.T. "Are human beings, as they are, in any way unfinished?"

H.H. In the spiritual sense?

R.T. Yes, and in the evolutionary sense also, perhaps. Have they reached the fulfillment of their evolution, perfected their brain and heart and understanding, or are they unfinished in that sense?

H.H. In that sense, I don't know. The human brain may develop or it may decrease. I am not at all sure.

R.T. But isn't a Buddha a being with a more developed brain?

*The doctrine of emptiness

© Christopher de Menlil

H.H. But that's not natural evolution.

R.T. Isn't it? It is not test tube development!

H.H. (*Gales of laughter.*) I think, you see, without effort, that kind of evolution we are speaking about cannot take place. For example, first an animal goes on four legs, then on two legs, then it is easier to run around, yes? Now that is without effort, isn't it?

R.T. I don't think it is without effort.

H.H. Not in the sense that, for example, those four-legged creatures needed some effort to go on two legs—that kind of effort, yes. But I speak of evolution in the Buddhist sense: for example, in the primordial eon, beings do not depend on grosser food. Then they go down, and finally reach a ten-year life span. That period is the worst the human race can reach. Then again another rise, and finally they reach the time of Maitreya's teaching. That we may call "evolution." And that without special effort.

R.T. I see what you mean.

H.H. Simply as you see the seasons changing, these are cycles. We are still, you see, on the line of decline. . . .

R.T. Unfortunately.

H.H. (*Laughing.*) You can't say unfortunately. That's just the way it is.

R.T. But, an individual who is reborn after an effort in his individual life—for example, one who creates the spirit of enlightenment, who conceives that higher mind—then he advances in evolution, even though he is in a world like this.

H.H. You see, the human level of mental development, of course, is not a finished one—even in the ordinary sense, within our inner state there are still many things to explore. This has nothing to do with religious ideology; this is spiritual. I think some part of the brain's capability may be fully utilized only through deep meditation. But meantime, there are certain things still to be explored in the ordinary way. So from that viewpoint, the human being is unfinished.

R.T. (*Laughing.*) Does Buddha have more brain, do you think, in his *ushṇisha?**

H.H. It is not a question of that. The grosser consciousness depends heavily on particles of matter; so it is the grosser level that has very much to do with the brain. The subtler consciousness is more independent. So the innermost subtle consciousness does not depend so much on the brain. If it did, it couldn't exist without the brain; and you see, in the Buddha state, the grosser mind completely disappears. Luminance, radiance, imminence—the three states of the subtle mind—all of these disappear in the clear light, the clear light of supreme innermost subtle consciousness.

*The cranial dome. Buddha's was unusually large.

R.T. Exactly, exactly!

Now: "What is the realization which the Whole Person enjoys?" Would you say, like Shāntideva, that the more a person is aware of others, the more they approach wholeness?

H.H. Right!

R.T. So in a sense, to a human being, compassion is almost natural.

H.H. Right, right. As I already said, there are many different levels of the Whole Person. For example, one sees a dog beaten by someone; a Whole Man, on a certain level, then feels a certain kind of pain. Although he is not beaten physically himself, yet mentally he feels he himself gets some kind of blow. If one sees a bug killed before one, one feels a shiver of identification.

R.T. Yes. So though people say that human beings are aggressive, like apes, like tigers, would you say rather that the essence of human nature was not aggression but compassion—differentiating him from the animal?

H.H. I think so. I think so. If the basic human nature was aggressive, we would have gotten animal claws and huge teeth—but ours are very short, very pretty, very weak! So that means we are not well equipped to be aggressive beings. Even the size of our mouths is very limited. So I think the basic nature of the human being should be gentle.

R.T. Now PARABOLA asks: "What does it mean to be free and open?"

H.H. I understand the meaning of "open" as just like open door: it can open very easily, without difficulty. Then "free," that is also the same. And as a result of being free and open, the more you receive new ideas, that makes you want to give out more your own energy. That way, I think, each helps the other. The more new ideas come, the more you see the way open for your own expression or thought to go out. That I think is very useful, very necessary, especially these days.

R.T. Don't you think "openness" is a matter of views, primarily—of not what we call "holding one's own view as superior"? For example, a prejudiced person, who thinks he already knows everything, is not exactly open, is he? So in a sense, doesn't "open" mean "free of wrong views"?

H.H. That's right. The more pride, the greater arrogance, then the less open one is. Yes, we do call that holding one's own belief as highest, not accepting other beliefs. Now, there is a different meaning there. The self realizes that our knowledge and our mental development are not fully developed, and feels that there are a lot of new things to be understood; in that sense one is open and free-minded. But there are certain things one investigated oneself, for a long time, and found a conclusion, with reason. On those subjects, you should be very firm. That does not mean you are not open-minded. But since you fully investigated, and you found the firm answer, you accept that as ultimately true. Openness does not mean you are wishy-washy, or that if someone comes and says, "Oh, this is not that," then you change; and another person says the opposite and again you change. It is not like that! Conceit about a view means a certain wrong view of reality, a dogmatic attitude. That is view-conceit. But holding truth as true, without prejudice—there is no pride there.

R.T. "How do you see openness in the sense of the non-obstruction of life-force?"

Coming back to fanaticism and dogmatism about views, there is the field of race-relations: "I am white," "I am black," "I am Chinese," "I am American." For such persons, even some little hints of emptiness might make their views more gentle and temper their fanatic ideology, don't you think? It might dawn on them that their deepest identity was something beyond their race or nationality.

H.H. Now, here, you see, two things are involved, so we should be very clear. There are two levels of the strong feeling that I am of this race of that race; one, the conventional level—just the mere recognition that "I am an Easterner" or "I am an American," which is true. There is nothing wrong with that. It is reality. In order to make harmony between races, the basis is difference; there are different types, and it is thus harmony comes. The realization of emptiness in no way harms this feeling. Even I think it supports it. Now this is the level of conventional recognition. Then there is another thing. With this realization, then the other strong feeling, the truth-habit, arises. When that joins this mere recognition, it starts trouble. It is that feeling that becomes racism; the prejudices of the truth-habit are very much involved. Now, the view of the realization of emptiness is quite contrary to that feeling of truth-habit; it is the antidote for that. For example, I see something good; I appreciate it, it's a good thing. Here there's nothing wrong. Then I go beyond that: "Oh, it is very beautiful!" and I become very much attached to it; then there is something wrong. So you see, the view realizing emptiness removes the exaggerated identity feeling on the second level, not on the first level. The first level, if we misapply emptiness on the conventional level of surface reality, then confusion will arise, nothing can be distinguished, then it will go into nihilism.

R.T. Yes; that's very precise. That's great. . . .

Now, another question. "I understand your teaching to say that the Buddha nature is inherent in every person. There is also an expression, especially in Zen Buddhism, 'effortless effort,' which is often misunderstood to mean an inner passivity. What kind of active inner effort is necessary for the liberation of the Whole Person within?"

H.H. This "effortless effort" is what is called the effortless striving. Right. Now in the meditation of mental quiescence, in the nine states of mind, there is a state where striving must be abandoned; an effortless concentration is necessary at a certain stage. It is effortless; that means, your mind becomes very tranquil—with good qualities, with its character complete. At that moment, if you make effort, that disturbs the tranquillity. So in order to maintain that pure tranquillity, the sort of effortless effort must be used. Of course, it is a kind of effort. You have to make at least a mental effort: "Now, I don't want to make effort!" That means effort, in order to have less disturbance of meditation.

R.T. So there's a kind of wisdom. . . .

H.H. No, not a kind of wisdom, a kind of concentration. Before this moment, when your mind tends to depression, then you need some effort to raise up your mind, intensify it. When your mind becomes active and ready to go to different objects in distraction, at that time your mind should be quieted. So that effort must be made. When your mind becomes even, with no more fluctuations, you need to stabilize it; that is the effortless effort. That is the simple effort to heighten any tendency to depression, lower any tendency to excitement. It is effortless in the sense of subtly balanced. It has nothing to do with emptiness. Of course you need an active inner effort.

R.T. "Can you explain what is meant by compassion and why it seems so little accessible?"

H.H. Now, our compassion is not just sheer emotion by itself. One must think over some reasons; it comes with reasons; thinking that all beings want happiness, do not want suffering; thinking over such reasons, wishing to free them from suffering.

R.T. Besides, from the Buddhist point of view, is it really "so little accessible"? Isn't it quite accessible for a human being?

H.H. Yes, it's not far away from human beings. Their using compassion depends on whether or not they know how to think it over, how to cultivate it in their minds, or whether they make effort. The key is how to use the mind, how to open the mind through reason, and then make the effort.

R.T. PARABOLA's next question: "Are lower energies to be purified in the sense of removed, or are they to be transformed? In what sense can the lower forces be a help?"

In other words, must the lower energies only be suppressed, or can they be carried into the path and be an actual help, if rightly treated?

H.H. Yes, they can, in some cases. I think the different stages must be considered. The initial, preliminary stage is when the person is not yet much developed in the wisdom field; during that time, the lower energies should be controlled. Then when there is more wisdom power, and also some other technique, then they can be transformed—so that the lower force becomes, instead of an obstacle, a help.

R.T. But if you try to do that too soon. . .

H.H. Without other factors, then by itself it will not work; it is dangerous. For instance, there are certain very powerful poisons, say morphine, which in certain cases can be used for medicine. Aryadeva, in one of his works, put up a great argument: "The various substances

enjoyed in the Tantric practice according to the vows, these things can be used in that practice . . . for example, poison can be used effectively as medicine. As it helps, it is no longer poison, but medicine. As it helps, it is to be used."

R.T. Now, "What would be a fruitful attitude for me to hold towards those things in myself which I would like to change? Should I hate these aspects of myself? Study them? Try to eliminate them? Learn to accept them?"

H.H. That depends on your own inner strength. There are different techniques. If it is someone who knows, and who has the capability, that is one thing; if not, the only thing is to eliminate. And after all, the ultimate aim is to eliminate these. But the method sometimes makes use of these negative forces; for example, insects born from wood eat the very wood—it's like that. Those persons who are using these lower energies or wrong thoughts—that does not mean they accept these thoughts, only that a different method is being used. It's something like wrathfully killing one's enemy in the open, or using stealth and deception to kill him; in both cases, the essential point is to kill the enemy. In one case, with a very wrathful face, in the other, a very polite one, and then exploiting his own weakness.

R.T. Yes, like judo.

H.H. Exactly.

R.T. Now they ask: "Is there a relationship with one's own suffering which is not usually understood?"

H.H. In Christian teaching, suffering has some powerful meaning, doesn't it? For example, Jesus took the suffering himself. Now that, you see, was not in the ordinary sense, but something very meaningful. Now in Buddhist tradition, we have every right to avoid, to overcome suffering; but when the suffering actually happens, then, instead of being discouraged or mentally distressed, you simply utilize that occasion in such a way that it will benefit you. For the moment, you will minimize your mental disturbance, and for the long run, you develop a certain kind of motivation that will help you to gain more virtue.

R.T. Your Holiness always says that suffering increases your inner strength.

H.H. That is right.

R.T. But some people might think: well, then, I should seek more suffering in order to become stronger.

H.H. (*Laughing.*) This I don't mean.

R.T. But voluntary suffering—in a way, isn't that what it is? Don't Bodhisattvas sometimes seek suffering on purpose?

H.H. Oh yes, they do. "I want to take on myself all the sufferings of living beings." They directly enter into suffering that way. But in that case, you see, actually the suffering does not come!

R.T. Ahh! Is that so? When they seek the suffering, they don't get any?

H.H. No, never. The wishing for suffering makes the suffering disappear.

R.T. That's beautiful.
Another question: "In light of the plurality of religious traditions living side by side in the world today, many people find it impossible to move wholeheartedly into any one tradition; such is the dilemma of modern Western man. Yet to draw a little from this tradition and a little from that seems too often to lead to a featureless pudding. What advice can you give to those in this predicament?"

H.H. What is "pudding"?

R.T. *Thugpa*—everything boiled down to a mush.

H.H. (*Laughing.*) Oh, oh, oh, oh. . . .
At the initial stage, I think there is nothing wrong in taking something from this tradition and other things from that tradition—not necessarily becoming a follower of a particular tradition but simply remaining as a good human being. I think that is possible; not only possible, I think it is good. Then if you want further development, a deeper level—it is like education. On the school level, you learn this subject a little, that subject a little. Then you become interested in one field; then you have to choose one particular subject, and train, and become an expert in that line. In the

spiritual line also, when you want to deepen your understanding and your experience, then you should follow one tradition. And develop.

R.T. Yes. I was struck yesterday by your use of the metaphor "spiritual supermarket" to mean something good; I thought it was very beautiful. Usually people use that expression to mean something bad, but you meant that a supermarket offers many choices, many options.

H.H. Ah-hah! Do they usually think of it as something bad? Why?

R.T. Precisely because of the idea that with a little bit of everything it will become *thugpa*, a hodgepodge, as in the question. But you turned it around, and I agree with your interpretation, definitely: "supermarket" means you have more possibility, more different kinds of people can get what they need. You're not stuck with the one thing they have in the little village store. That's wonderful, and it applies here.

Now, "What advice would you give to an ordinary Western man or woman who is concerned about discovering his or her true inner nature?"

H.H. I think, to try to get at least some time, with quiet and relaxation, to think more inwardly and to investigate the inner world. That may help. Then sometimes, when one is very much involved in hatred or attachment, if there is time or possibility during that very moment, just try to look inward: "What is attachment? What is the nature of anger?" That also is good.

R.T. "What is the proper relationship of knowledge to feeling in one's search for the Whole Person within, and what role does the body play in this search?" In other words, is intellectual understanding helpful at all, or is it just an obstacle?

H.H. Ah, but you see, generally speaking, the intellect is not at all an obstacle for searching inner truth. But certain experiences are reached at certain times without using the intellectual side, simply through a kind of direct feeling; that also is possible, from the Buddhist viewpoint. But usually, reasonings are essential. Nevertheless, when you practice the path of Unexcelled Yoga Tantra, when you cultivate the bliss-void-indivisible samadhi, you don't practice analytic meditation, you proceed by concentrative, non-discursive meditation alone. It's the same with the Great Perfection and Great Soul teachings. Now that does not mean the intellect is fundamentally useless. These are different times and different circumstances.

R.T. Especially during the time of learning and reflection prior to meditation. You can't just proceed on faith.

H.H. That's it.

R.T. So would you say that intellectual knowledge initially is crucial?

H.H. Yes. And then in connection with the role of the body, you see, when intellectual work is carried on, the brain and its physical particles are very much involved. So you see usually these intellectual thoughts are a grosser level of mind, which is very much connected with the cell particles. In a state wherein the grosser mind becomes inactive, then the subtler mind becomes more active, and at that moment the relation of the subtler mind and the body cells is left behind, so at that time the intellectual work is also left behind.

Now there are two ways: one method is the meditation of non-thinking—these are the methods of the Great Perfection and Great Seal. Through the non-conception practice, one should reach clear light. There are other methods, through *tummo* heat yoga, through *Vajra* incantation, through breathing practice and so on. But in every case, in the initial stage, the other factor must be there. Even for the practice of the Great Perfection, it requires renunciation, it requires the spirit of enlightenment. Again now, the intellectual function is indispensable.

I don't know the exact meaning of the word "intellect" in English, but if it is our Tibetan *togpa*, conceptual thought, then the decision, "I am going to meditate in a thoughtless state," is itself a thought.

R.T. Could one use the simile of shooting a gun? Your sight, aiming at the target, is the concept. To hit the target you must sight accurately, have the right concept. The actual shooting is not a concept; the bullet just goes where it is aimed. So that is the non-conceptual concentration. But of course, the aiming is crucial. Is that a fair example?

H.H. Yes, that's fine. It's quite useful. . . . Of course, there are still some problems. When we talk of the thoughtless state, we are talking really of a deeper level.

© Christopher de Menil

R.T. Yes, of course.

The next question is: "What Buddhist concepts are most misunderstood by Westerners, and what troubles you most about the consequences of this misunderstanding?"

H.H. I think *shūnya* is one of them, and also some Tantric practices; and something like "the blood-drinking deities."

R.T. (*Laughing.*) Cannibal activity!

© *Christopher de Menil*

H.H. For example, Vajrabhairava, the tutelary deity, is very easy to misunderstand; it really looks like some kind of devil. And one can only slowly understand its function as a symbol of the union of the wisdom of great bliss and voidness after an awful lot of explanations. Otherwise it is very misunderstandable. And sex!

R.T. Yes, certainly; there was a lot of confusion about Tantra based on poorly translated Hindu sources.

H.H. What is troubling is the simple fact of the misunderstanding preventing people from getting the right idea. Some people who don't really know anything and pretend to know a lot about it cause the most trouble. And if it is thought that Tibetan Buddhism is some kind of strange business, this is very harmful to Tibetans, as it makes people not respect their culture and so not defend their human rights, not cry out against their national tragedy.

R.T. Now it is asked: "Are true religious teachings fragile? Is the greatest threat to their potency and vigor from inside or from outside? And if from inside, what are the threats?"

R.T. I don't think religious teaching is easy to wipe out, but very difficult. Once it is deep-rooted, I don't think it is easy to destroy. The actual threat comes from the inside. That means, you see, those so-called "religious persons" who do not practice well, do not follow a proper way. That is the most dangerous, the greatest threat. In our own Tibetan case, there is the outside threat. Of course, it can easily destroy the temples and monasteries, but it is very difficult to destroy the inner feeling. But suppose one Tibetan monk or lama behaves badly, then that can do very much harm. That can really destroy the inner faith, the inner feeling. So the actual threat comes from within. And also, using religion as the instrument for division; that also is a threat. And then I think in some cases, you yourself can have too much attachment to the ideology and lose the basic aim of religion, of helping humankind.

R.T. We come to the last question: "What is the task of the Whole Man, and what fundamental questions are you concerned with in relation to your sojourn on earth?"

H.H. The task of the Whole Man is to help others; that's my firm teaching. That is my own belief. For me, the fundamental question is better relations, better relations among human beings—and whatever I can contribute to that.

17

◆

An Interview with Helen M. Luke

"Wholeness," VOL. X:1, February, 1985

Letting Go

Helen Luke was born in 1904 in England. She received a Masters degree in French and Italian literature from Somerville College, Oxford. Twenty years later, she became interested in the work of C.G. Jung, and studied his thought in Zurich and London. Arriving in the United States in 1949, she established a practice as a counselor in Los Angeles. Today her work continues through her writings—Crossroad has published three collections of her essays, including Woman: Earth and Spirit, The Inner Story, and most recently, The Voice Within—and at the Apple Farm Community, begun in 1962 near Three Rivers, Michigan.

Apple Farm has been described as a "center for people seeking to discover and appropriate the transforming power of symbols in their lives," and as a "women's contemplative community." Neither of these descriptions convey the impressions which begin to gather during even a brief visit. It is clear that the steadily growing number of people who settle near Apple Farm are deeply committed to what Jung termed "the way of individuation." Perhaps this is why it seems to be a community without any of the pejorative implications of a group. One meets individuals, breathing free air, finding their own way. It is Helen Luke's own deep search, the warmth and vision which have grown from it, and her uncompromising respect for the dignity of the individual which make the unique atmosphere of Apple Farm possible—and the special quality of her words in the interview which follows.

253

PARABOLA You expressed some uneasiness when I told you the theme of this interview, and suggested that it might be better if we spoke of "Approaching Wholeness." Why is that?

HELEN LUKE I think my feeling is that very few people in any generation do actually come to what we would call wholeness incarnate. There may be a lot more who do so just before they die. But as long as we are in linear time, it cannot be put into words, or talked about really by anyone who is still on the way. There are moments for all of us, I think, when we break out beyond that and have a glimpse of what it is, but the few great ones—those whom the East would call Buddhas, whom we would call those who live the Christ within all the time—are very, very, rare. But they do exist. And I do think we should talk about our intuitions of wholeness. This is very important in the beginning. Once one knows it is there, one can be absolutely certain of meaning in life—and go along whatever one's way is, trying to remember. We're so apt to forget.

P. It's curious what it is in us which does remember.

H.L. There is something which remembers—it's always there. I don't think anyone who has once experienced it would ever forget entirely. Although it can turn negative.

P. In what way?

H.L. When it's swallowed up by a power drive from the ego.

P. The glimpse itself can become an obstacle?

H.L. Well, wholeness must include everything. It is our choice as human beings as to whether we experience it positively or negatively. You may have read Charles Williams's *Descent Into Hell*. It's so clear there that Wentworth, who ends up in a state of hell, does so by small choices along the way. He is absorbed *into* wholeness, though he as a unique person no longer exists. After all, Dante made it very clear that hell is a choice. People who were in his Hell, if offered Heaven, would not and could not choose it.

P. You have written that people do get what it is that they want. Why do you think it is that so few seem to choose the path toward wholeness—

that so many choose peace, perhaps, rather than struggle?

H.L. It could be said, I think, that we all try to choose peace, but that many move further and further away from it by evasion of the struggles and necessary conflicts of the human journey. What the one on the way to hell chooses all the time is peace for himself: rejection of everybody else except for his own ego; like Wentworth, he chooses his own images of a lover instead of an actual lover, and so on. The point about peace is that the true peace does not come until one has been through *all* the struggles of the ego, and until one has accepted boundaries and conflict—to the bitter end. That's what the whole Christian story is about. That's what the cross is.

P. Jung has written that what we call consciousness is just a tiny island in the vast and deep sea of the psyche, and that man is a small part of the whole and can never really know it. So we are limited in many ways.

H.L. Yes, because we are still centered in the ego, you see: I find it very interesting that you are doing this issue on "Wholeness" after your first issue which was on "The Hero." We all have to experience at first the strengthening of the ego, the development of its ability to discriminate, to make choices, to get into trouble, to get out of it, and so on. And then comes a point when one has to sacrifice the hero. The hero himself has had to make his sacrifices along the way in order to defeat the dragon, to achieve his aim. Now this in Jungian terms would be the journey of the ego getting to know its shadow side—all the parts that have been repressed, both good and bad. It isn't that the shadow is only the dark elements which we think are wicked, because one can also repress one's positive abilities if one does not want to take the responsibility of living them. But there comes a time when the ego relatively knows all it can, has come to terms with its dark sides, can recognize when it is being possessed by projections, and so on. And when that work is largely done—and this I think is a very important moment on Jung's way of individuation, as he called it—there comes a time when we must sacrifice the will to achieve, the time when we then have to let go. It's what Lao Tzu says—that when you are pursuing learning you gain something every day, but when you turn to the Tao—which means wholeness, really—then you drop something every day, you let go of something every day. It's a letting-go process, and it takes usually many years, letting go by degrees. For instance, if you don't begin to let go of your will to be successful, to achieve in the outer world—or, for that matter, in the inner world too—the ego will go on saying that you must get better and better every day. What begins that process of letting go is when you can really experience the difference between the ego—that little light of consciousness that we have—and the Self, which is the whole Self, the whole sphere and also the center. The Self is a Jungian term, in India it is the Atman, and in the West the Christ within, the divine wholeness both immanent in every unique human being and at the same time transcendent and universal. If you are still identified with the ego, after you have had a glimpse of the Self, then you may begin to be possessed by a drive for power even if you weren't before. This is how so many cults develop. The leader had a very real vision at one time as a young man, but then he begins to teach it and it becomes identified with his personal ego. Now in each of us this can easily happen, to some degree.

P. In the hero's journey, then, it is necessary to develop the ego very strongly so that there is then something which can let go?

H.L. Exactly; through the ego's choices the inner vision becomes incarnate. In a recent book by Russell Lockhart, *Words as Eggs*, he asks in the introduction, what are we to do after we have done the absolutely necessary work of coming to terms with the shadow, with the "animus" and "anima," the masculine in a woman, the feminine in a man, the inner figures? We can now recognize them and know when one of them starts playing tricks—what do we do then? It seems that very often psychologists are not clear when the religious side must take over; not in the literal church sense, but in the deepest spiritual sense.

P. In all your work I feel a kind of interdependence between the way of Jung, turning to what is dark, what is hidden, and the Christian way of turning toward the light of Logos. I don't know if you feel this is so.

H.L. Yes, but when you say the light of Logos, do you mean God? Well, don't call it Logos, because the Self is not just Logos, it is Eros as well, and indeed, the Self is the unity of opposites. It is the truth of Christianity, too, but you rightly say that Christians so often mistake the light of Logos for the whole. Jung pointed out the absolute necessity for the feminine values without which there would be no perception of Self. This is especially true in our time when everything is geared toward achievement. One of the best antidotes to that is to read Lao Tzu, I think: "When you do nothing, everything is done." And it's true—if you are talking on the right level. But it's mostly not understood. You see, it is so much a matter of levels. Of course cause and effect and all that comes from them operate in our daily lives on that level the whole time. But it cannot really have a meaning—and that's our great danger—unless we recognize that time itself doesn't exist. That's what physicists are now telling us. It is a very exciting thing in our time, modern physics, which is confirming everything that the East has known for thousands of years.

P. The fact that something can be true on one level, and utterly false on another, causes a great deal of confusion, I think. And also the inaccessibility of a level higher than one is on.

H.L. Yes. The point of the second half of life, then, is to discover that level which makes all the other levels distinct, yet one in the whole. I have seen as I get *really* old that something fascinating begins to happen. As everybody knows, you begin to remember early things in your life very vividly—and then you are apt to forget things that happened yesterday because they're not important anymore somehow. My view is that you do remember things that are really vital, but you forget much that isn't. At any rate, you remember the early things. And then there is, so to speak, a choice: you can either let that state, as so many people naturally do, become nostalgia, or even senility, or it's possible that those memories suddenly acquire an enormously enhanced meaning in the whole of your life; and you begin to see your life as a circle instead of as a straight line. That's just one place where you begin to find that level where everything is a circle. But we have to walk on the straight lines, and we have to experience fully the horizontal and the vertical, the earth and the spirit, and the meeting point at the center before that can happen.

P. In Castaneda's book, Don Juan called old age the last enemy, and your description of how that last enemy is overcome is quite different from images of fighting against it, denying it—or simply sinking into it. You are saying that it is a time for continuing to grow—a very important kind of new growth.

H.L. That's the vital thing, and you can only do that by letting things go, not by holding on. It comes, in my experience, little by little, in allowing outer responsibilities to drop away at the right times. But more and more—and I think this is most important—it becomes a matter of turning our attention to the smallest things. I can so easily feel that I have to get over with washing the dishes or whatever needs doing around the house in order to get down to doing what is really important— to sit down and write, or meditate, or whatever! After you let go the hero who wants to kill the dragon and go out and conquer, the task becomes a matter of full attention to the smallest fact. And you can catch yourself rejecting a fact. Over and over. Whether it is the fact of this table, or the fact of having slipped and fallen, or whatever may happen to you, or the world, or anything else, but also the fact of the chair you're sitting in. The whole either doesn't exist, or it exists in everything. We are forever trying to exclude the ego's failures—to exclude in order to find our peace that way. But to find our peace by including everything, dark and light, is a very great suffering for the ego, because it has to give up all its will to dominate. The ego doesn't get any weaker; in fact, it probably gets a lot stronger, and the darkness becomes greater. But both are facts. And without both, one cannot come near to that level where wholeness can be lived—at least some of the time!

P. Gurdjieff said, "The bigger the angel, the bigger the devil."

H.L. Exactly so. Wasn't it Rilke who refused to go to see Freud or to go into analysis because he said that they might take away his devils, but they'd also take away his angels? And that's true, with most analysis. It can happen when analysis is geared to making someone feel good in the world, adjusted and all the rest. That's the great difference in Jung—he's not concerned about whether you are terribly well adjusted in the world, because what he's interested in is the psyche in its relationship to the Self. The ego is terribly important—it's still a complex, it's still there—but it can become one with the Self without losing its uniqueness. That's the marvelous thing.

P. I have a question here about how words can mean such different things, for example relationship and dependence which on the one hand can mean an excuse and an escape—to lose oneself in relationship with another, to escape responsibility in dependence. On the other hand there is true relationship and real dependence arising from the facts you were just speaking of. Related to this is the child, who appears to have a kind of wholeness and integrity, and the adult, who seems to have to go through a process of fragmentation and division before the meaning of relationship and dependence can become so utterly different.

H.L. Yes, that really is the point. The enormous difference is that when you begin to know yourself and to glimpse the Self—the wholeness in which all relationship is free and yet essential—you are no longer relating through projection. The child is simply unconsciously one with the wholeness of everything. As soon as it begins to say "I," then comes the beginning of that kind of dependence which is projection. There is a kind of magical attraction from the unconscious. You are part of an archetypal situation—mother and child, and so on. The work of gaining consciousness is to free yourself from identification with one person or another. If you find you hate a person or that there is something that makes you absolutely furious, you may be perfectly sure that it is a part of yourself that is projected there—no matter how true it may be that the other person is behaving badly. You could see that without getting all het up about it. It's normal that one should be angry at things that go on, but there's quite a different quality in that anger if you have ceased to project. If you are projecting you are incapable of compassion, you are incapable of understanding that this person is behaving in this way for reasons that you cannot see, from problems that you know nothing about, but that we all share.

P. Just to be sure I'm clear here, projection is really a kind of identification of yourself with the other?

H.L. And you don't do it deliberately. It just happens. Projection is the way you see everything that is unconscious in yourself. If you didn't have that projection, you'd never see it. You wouldn't even know you had it. Once you begin to take projections back, this magical kind of tie changes. Once you begin to let go—and this takes a great deal of hard work and watching, and attention and humility; when once you can ask what is it in me that *must* have this to depend on—the minute you begin to make that separation between yourself and that projection, it may then become a sense of relationship. This is so even if it is a relationship with something you dislike and will go on disliking—no one is trying to tell you that you ought to feel differently in that sense—but it will also be compassionate. That, I believe, is what the East means by saying all is emptiness, all is compassion. Not just emptiness—nothing there—but filled with compassion, which is a suffering with whatever is involved. You see the difference? It doesn't mean you can do without relationship: very much the opposite. But you recognize that relationship cannot happen until you are separate. Otherwise it is just a mixup in the unconscious of two people. You have to separate in order to unite, because uniting means two unique things that meet. Not two fuzzy things—that merge!

That gradual letting go still has to have a context. I think it's enormously important to realize as we work with dreams and the unconscious and other people do the same kind of work in different ways, that when you have an insight it's not enough just to understand. It has then somehow to be put into actual life. It has to be incarnate. This is the true meaning of Christianity. Someone will say he or she has had a big dream and that she feels what it means and so on—she or he must do *something* with it, write it down, paint it, do something *in this world* with it, and after that let it take effect in daily life. It has to make a change, however tiny. This is nearly always a letting go of something. It's all a preparation, of course, for the final letting go of death.

P. You have written something about forgiveness that I wanted to ask you about. You wrote, ". . . it is the breakthrough of forgiveness, in its most profound sense—universal and particular, impersonal and personal— that alone brings the 'letting go,' the ultimate freedom of the spirit. For in the moment of that realization every false guilt, whether seen as one's own or as other people's, is gone forever—and the real guilt which each of us carries, of refusal to see, to be aware, is accepted. So we may look open-eyed at ourselves and the world and suffer the pain and joy of the divine conflict which is the human condition, the meaning of reincarnation." It seems that something must appear to make this possible, to make one *able*.

H.L. It may appear in something that happens to you, comes to you from the outer world, or it may appear from something that comes to you suddenly from the inner world. It will happen through a long history of choices in small things. The unwillingness to see is to say "no" to life, to the risk of mistakes, to facts.

P. Do you think that with all the difficulties something helps as well?

H.L. Oh, but of course! The difficulties are what help most!

P. I mean that the right difficulties are brought to you at the right time.

H.L. I think that if one has faith in the meaning of life at all, that is a certainty.

P. It's all arranged?

H.L. I don't like the word arranged. It just *is*. It's your fate, and you have a choice how to live it. The East would call it your karma.

P. I have a question about what is really one's own. Certainly all the energies of youth are given, one's talents, weaknesses, and so on are given, but they all seem like raw material. Is there something at the end which could be there and have the taste of being one's own?

H.L. Your own—how do you mean that? That seems to be a matter of discrimination in the use of words. How does St. Paul put it? "Having nothing, yet possessing all things." Now I would rather have it the other way round, as possessing nothing, yet having all things, because there are so many negative meanings to possession. But it means the same thing, of course. In the ultimate wholeness we surely have everything, but we don't have it exclusively. It isn't ours and not somebody else's. That's the difference, and that is the letting go. You don't any longer feel, "I have the right to this." You don't have rights, you don't have demands, you don't have wishes. No, that's not true, your ego has them all the time! Don't think you are going to lose your ego's carryings-on; you're not. You merely are not moved by them in the old way. Less and less are they the center of your life. They operate on a certain level, but they become less and less demanding—of people, of things, of everything. Meister Eckhart said we must let go even of the demand to know God. Then it becomes yours. Then it is given to you—when it is completely let go.

P. Well, there seems to be some sort of task that we have in the course of our lives, and there must be an enormous difference between a person who achieves this aim and one who does not. As we are, this remains only a possibility in us.

H.L. It's a possibility, and it is enormously important for the whole world that some individuals grow to a deep and full consciousness.

P. Is there something which characterizes the way towards this?

H.L. I think there is something that one can notice in one's own life very clearly. There comes a point when an utterly different kind of suffering is possible, not a neurotic suffering. At the same time that one begins to move beyond the hero/villain stage, one no longer goes up and down into exaltations or depressions. It is the kind of suffering that comes when you accept the fact of whatever it is; a depression is when you don't accept the fact. The suffering which is not a depression can bring a deeper darkness, but it doesn't affect your behavior or those around you. The weight is gone, because there will also be a kind of joy that goes with it, which is nothing emotional. There is a possibility to move beyond being dominated by your emotions. That's the mistake people always make—we think we always have to be improving the ego. We don't. We have to put it through its journey of knowing itself and understanding itself, and so on, and then we shall recognize that its emotions are not objective. They are purely subjective, which is a necessary stage. But then comes what Jung calls objective cognition, and the kind of love he writes about in his autobiography, *Memories, Dreams, Reflections*. The love that is beyond all desiring, all emotions; and that is whole in itself because nothing is excluded.

P. Feeling without emotion?

H.L. None of these words somehow express it because it is a state of being, a state of the soul. In fact it is reality itself. But one just glimpses these things, now and then.

P. It is a long way from the way compassion is sometimes understood— as a sea of emotionality.

H.L. The feeling of wishing to save the world comes very often out of a wish to escape from having compassion on your own darkness, for what is inside yourself. If you don't start there you will never have true compassion. First comes compassion for your own weaknesses, and then for the person next to you. Now that doesn't mean that we shouldn't support causes—what matters is *who* supports the causes. You may have to fight, but if you don't fight with forgiveness and compassion, you simply are recreating the same situation. One opposite always creates the other, unless you begin to let go of both of them, then both can become real in a unity which is beyond them.

P. What you say brings to mind the words of Dame Julian of Norwich which you've just written about. "All shall be well by the purification of the motive in the ground of our beseeching."

H.L. That's really the point, isn't it—"By the purification of the motive. . . ." Actually this quotation is from T.S. Eliot's "Four Quartets." The motive—that which moves us from the very ground of our being—is slowly purified here in time through the individual's commitment to the emptying process which is the quest of wholeness. Then, in Lady Julian's words, "All shall be well, and all manner of thing shall be well."